A
WOMAN'S
VOICE

EDDIE ROWLEY

O'BRIEN PRESS
DUBLIN

DEDICATION

For Patricia and Kate

First published 1993 by The O'Brien Press Ltd.,
20 Victoria Road, Dublin 6, Ireland.

Copyright © text Eddie Rowley

10   9   8   7   6   5   4   3   2   1

British Library Cataloguing-in-publication Data.
A catalogue reference is available for this book at the British Library.

ISBN 0-86278-360-7

Cover design: Michael O'Brien
Design and layout: The O'Brien Press
Cover separations: The City Office, Dublin
Printing: The Guernsey Press Co. Ltd., Channel Islands

Acknowledgements

Special thanks to my *Sunday World* chiefs and colleagues: Editor
Colin McClelland, for his support; News Editor Sean Boyne, who has
shaped me as a writer and journalist and encouraged me to write my
first book; Des Ekin for his advice; Sarah Hamilton for all the
background information; and photographers Val Sheehan and
Mitchel O'Connor. Thanks also to Jackie Hayden of *Hot Press* for his
assistance; to the managers of all the artistes and to Lynne Fitzgerald
and Lindsey Holmes of Brookham PR, to record company personnel
and my fellow music writers who are quoted in the book. Thanks also
to Justin Green for his advice. Finally, thanks to Michael O'Brien, Ide
O'Leary, Frances Power and all the staff at the O'Brien Press for their
support and for making it an enjoyable experience.   *Eddie Rowley*

WOMAN'S
VOICE

CONTENTS

PROLOGUE

During the summer of 1992, an album released by a small Dublin record label took the Irish music industry by storm. *A Woman's Heart* focused on the varied musical styles of six female artistes from the home scene. Music lovers were enthralled by the collection of performers, songs and music. Their phenomenal demand has made *A Woman's Heart* the biggest-selling album of all time in Ireland, with sales in excess of 200,000 copies. It has also served to draw attention to the talented women who figure on that particular album.

Some are long-established performers. Others are relative newcomers. In this book, the reader will be taken backstage and into the private lives of the album's six performers: Mary Black, Frances Black, Eleanor McEvoy, Dolores Keane, Maura O'Connell and Sharon Shannon. I have also selected two additional artistes of the same calibre, Máire Brennan of Clannad and Mary Coughlan, in order to give a comprehensive picture of how women have made the breakthrough to stardom on the music scene, sometimes against seemingly impossible odds. *A Woman's Voice* strips away the glamour and glitz to explore the reality of life on the road for a female singer and musician struggling to become established. It tells how the women, many of whom are mothers and wives, have juggled a career and family life. While the performance is obviously the most important feature as far as the fans are concerned and the most enjoyable aspect of the career for the artiste, the individual biographies reveal how that is only part of what a performer has to contend with. This book depicts the devastating blows an entertainer can suffer along the route to stardom. It reveals how singers and musicians also have to get to grips with the business side of their career to survive in what is often regarded as a shark-infested industry. And it shows how luck – being in the right place at the right time and coming to the attention of the right person – can play a major role in launching or consolidating a performer's career.

Although many of the artistes have been around for a long time, their early lives have never before been documented in detail. The performers have also opened their private family photographic albums to allow the reader a peek at the various stages, events and situations in their lives. This book does not pretend to be the definitive version of each performer's career. But with the aid of special interviews with the eight stars and a comprehensive survey of other interviews they have given in recent years, I have attempted to get to know each one of them. I hope that at the end of the book, you will feel you know them too.

MARY BLACK

MARY BLACK

Madonna has done it. Tina Turner has done it. Cher has done it. They're all women who have beaten the odds to notch up phenomenal achievements, both artistically and financially, in showbusiness. But few women in Ireland would perceive them as role models. Their world seems far removed from the environment that most women inhabit. Somehow, it's hard to image any of these people coping with the demands of a family and home while, at the same time, juggling a high-flying career. A picture of Madonna bringing in a bucket of coal from the back yard hours after playing a concert at Dublin's Point Depot, seems an even more bizarre possibility than some of the outrageous antics she has trotted out in her day.

But if women need a role model to spur them on in their drive to realise burning ambitions, there is one Irish artiste who fits easily into that mould – Mary Black. She is the all-round successful Irish woman. Marriage, children and a singing career, known around the world ... she has it all. And she has never sacrificed any of her principles or her self-respect to achieve it. When you meet her, it's obvious that fame hasn't altered her likeable, down-to-earth personality. The rich Dublin tones and easy laugh are still there. There is a depth and warmth to her that betrays a genuine love of her music and singing.

In the fickle world of showbusiness, Mary Black is an enduring performer. She has never been a fashion-driven artiste, the one-hit wonder who disappears overnight. Like any career that has lasting quality, Mary started out in a low-key way and served

her apprenticeship, performing on the live circuit around Ireland. 'I've been around for a very long time,' she admits. 'I'm
not an overnight success and usually the ones who build
something gradually are more inclined to stay there a little bit
longer and I hope to do that.' She has a steely, but not ruthless,
determination that has kept her career running like a well-oiled
engine and constantly overcome the barriers down through the
years. She could so easily have allowed the demands of motherhood to take over her life and drop her career into a lower
gear, but, in fact, being a mother has made Mary even more
determined to run a double life successfully.

In an *Irish Times* interview she told Victoria White: 'I would
encourage any woman who's had a child and who's saying, "It's
going to be harder now," to say, "Right, it's not going to tie me
down. I can manage to have this child and bring it up properly
and still have a life of my own." My career only took off from
the time my first child was born and it kind of made me even
more determined to push my career as far as it would go. People
seem to think: Oh, she's married, settled, has a child, that's the
end of her. That made me more determined and more stubborn
about it and I said No. I started to work much more after Conor
[now aged 12] was born. Not that I wanted to get away from
him. I was absolutely bowled over by being a mother. I think
it's the most amazing experience of any woman's life – but I
kind of wanted to prove myself for him as well, and I wanted to
leave something for him. Then I managed to have two more
children and I continued to work. I toured America when I was
four months pregnant. And I was back on stage seven weeks
after my daughter was born. If you've got good help and you've
got a solid head on your shoulders and you think about things,
you can do it.'

Mary Black was only fifteen years old when she performed
in her first group, Terrace. The folk outfit consisted of her
brothers Shay and Michael, and two friends, John White, now

a Dublin bus driver/conducter, and Paschal Bermingham, whose current source of work is unknown to her. 'Before that,' Mary told me in an interview for this book, 'we would have been singing at sessions. But my first public gig would have been with Terrace. It wasn't a real serious band. We knew we weren't going to take the world by storm. But we enjoyed playing together. We'd play down in the Universal in Parnell Square and the Coffee Kitchen in Molesworth Street, little folk clubs around Dublin. We were also taken on for the occasional party. A cheese-and-wine party in the Montrose Hotel in Dublin was my very first gig. I was terrified and I forgot the words of the songs.'

Prior to that, Mary's singing had been encouraged at school. She went to St Louis Convent, Rathmines, and was a member of the choir there. She had also been in the Young Dublin Singers. Later, when her brother Shay was posted to Castlebar, County Mayo, while working with a telephone company, Mary used to join him at weekends. 'Shay got to know a lot of the musicians in the town and we'd be singing day and night. We were just mad for music. It was suggested to us then that we should get together and start up a proper band and record an album. That's what we did, and General Humbert was formed. It was 1975 and we recorded our first album, named after the group. We were very green and it was done on a very low budget. Nevertheless, it was an important part of the whole process of what was to come. The other members of the group were Shay Kavanagh on guitar, Rory Sommers on *uileann* pipes, John Donegan on mandolin and keyboards, Stevie Dunford on *bodhrán* and I was the singer. We did a six-week tour of Germany and we played a bit around Ireland. Although there was an awareness of us, it never really took off. We were well known in and around Castlebar and Dublin. In Dublin we played gigs in places like Tailors' Hall. At that stage, there were a lot of folk clubs on the go in the city. We disbanded about

eighteen months after we made the first album. But then Gael
Linn approached us and asked if we'd be interested in doing an
album. The lads were particularly keen on doing it because we
always thought the first album had been done without a lot of
thought going into it. The lads felt they had a lot more to offer
and they wanted to make one for posterity because they knew
we wouldn't be getting back together. They asked me to do it
with them and I felt it would be nice to leave something behind
that we would be more pleased with. So we did the album
General Humbert II, for Gael Linn and it's something I'm proud
of. I haven't got copies of either album myself, but when I was
in Japan some of the fans there had them. Japanese fans are
fanatical. They make sure they get copies of everything that you
ever recorded.'

After General Humbert, Mary says she 'drifted' for a couple
of years. 'I was singing with my brothers, Shay, Michael and
Martin. Frances was still a bit young. We went off to America
and busked around the East Coast for a couple of months. It was
an incredible experience and we became very professional.
Back home, I continued to get on with my life generally. I was
doing one or two gigs a month, but it wasn't a fully-fledged solo
career. I sang with Gerry O'Beirne [now a member of Sharon
Shannon's band]. In fact, the first major turning point for me
was doing a programme in the series *Christy Moore and Friends*
on RTE television in 1980. It was recorded at the Abbey Tavern
in Howth and Christy asked me to be a guest on the show. Gerry
O'Beirne and myself got together and did it. I missed the show
the day it was transmitted because it was the day I got married.
From that series came the album *Christy Moore and Friends*,
and I had the song, 'Anachie Gordon', on that. That really
brought me to a much wider audience. Straight away people
were beginning to ask: Who is this Mary Black? Has she made
an album? But there was nobody banging on the door trying to
record me.'

Mary's new husband, Joe O'Reilly, was working in the Dolphin record label at the time. He suggested that they should record Mary. 'I was a bit apprehensive about that because the Dolphin label was very much a ballad label. It had the Wolfe Tones, the Dublin City Ramblers, Paddy Reilly, which are all fine, but it's not what I do. I was worried about getting an image as another ballad singer, so I suggested that we start a new label and that's how Dara was born. It was the second record label and also the second generation – Joe's father had started Dolphin.'

A year after his TV series, Christy Moore asked Mary to support him at the National Concert Hall where he was doing a couple of concerts. 'I was really flattered. He was always very decent like that. He would give people a leg up if he felt they had talent and needed a bit of help. There was nothing in it for him. I said I'd love to do it, but my brothers Shay and Michael were away and I wasn't working with a guitar player at the time. He said Declan Sinnott was playing with him and he probably wouldn't mind doing a few songs with me. Something really happened that night. Dec and I just clicked and it was special – we both knew that we wanted to work more together. Shortly after that we began talking about doing an album that he would produce. That's how it all started in 1981.'

Declan Sinnott is still Mary's producer and co-arranger. 'He has had a huge influence on my career, but I think we complement each other in a lot of ways. Up to that time, Declan didn't have a lot of experience with traditional singers or a traditional way of approaching a song. He had been playing electric guitar with Moving Hearts and Horslips. He was more into the rock area of music, rhythm and blues. But he was keen on playing acoustic guitar again and this was an opportunity for him. We bounced off each other very well. I had a lot to learn from him and he was very keen to work with me. I had listened to all kinds of music growing up. But because of the folk revival at the time,

I had been sticking mostly to folk music. The collaboration with Declan gave me the opportunity to explore new areas of music. We are together now almost twelve years and the music has developed in its own way.

'The first album, the *Mary Black* album, was a collection of songs that I had been singing, with the exception of one or two. The second album, *Without The Fanfare*, was more of an expression of how we felt musically and was more of a statement. I was desperately trying to shake off the folk singer image, which used to drive me crazy. Although folk and traditional Irish music have had a huge influence on me and I would never turn my back on that, I didn't want to be confined to one area of music. I wanted to explore. I wanted to sing other kinds of songs and get into other kinds of music. I think the idea of doing an album of all original songs by songwriters who had previously not recorded any of their stuff was a good idea. We experimented with different instruments and more of an American sound. We needed to do that to know – to step back and look at the whole picture. When it came to the album *By The Time It Gets Dark*, we really felt our vision had settled and for the first time we knew exactly where we were going. It all began to fall into place properly.'

While getting to grips with a solo career, Mary Black was also fitting in performances with The Black Family and De Danann. 'There were a lot of different things happening in my life at the same time. We recorded *The Black Family* around 1986/1987. Everyone was home for Christmas. Michael had come back from America and Shay was over from England. We'd been singing together and it sounded better than ever, and Joe [Mary's husband] suggested that we should record an album to put down what we had been doing and to have it there on record for the future. There was no big plan. We all knew we would do our own thing and there was no way we were getting together to form something. But the attitude was that it would be an album to have for our grandchildren. So we went in and very, very quickly, over a period of four or five days, put down all the songs that we had been doing for a couple of years. We recorded it very much in a live kind of way, in that we all got up and sang together. We didn't layer on different voices at different times.

'When the album came out the reaction was just great. We couldn't believe it. That same Christmas we had done the *Late Late Show* with Gay Byrne and there had been a huge reaction to it. We sang a couple of songs and had a bit of a chat with Gay. People knew that we were recording at that stage, so the interest was there. The following Christmas when we got together again, we organised eight or ten gigs around Ireland, including two shows at the Olympia Theatre in Dublin. It was sold out everywhere. But we all knew it was something we couldn't really pursue. I was very involved in my own career and I felt that it [The Black Family] was confusing the issue again. I had been working to try and establish myself as a contemporary singer and here I was falling back into the folky thing again. But my memories of that time together are very special, and I know there will be opportunities to get together again in the future.

'I joined De Danann in 1983 and I was with them until 1986. I released my solo album *Without The Fanfare* during that time. I was also working with Declan doing solo work. It had been cleared before I joined De Danann. I said: "Look, I'd love to be in the band, but if and when we are not working would you object to me working with Declan Sinnott?" They told me there was no problem. With every solo album I did the interest was growing and the pressure was there to do more solo work, so it was inevitable that I would eventually leave. But De Danann was invaluable as regards gaining experience. I was away on the road for long periods of time, working all over Europe and America. Up till then, I hadn't worked very much outside Ireland. And, of course, it brought me to a broader audience and people started to get to know my name.'

At the time, De Danann consisted of Frankie Gavin, Alec Fin, Mairtín O'Connor and Johnny McDonagh. Dolores Keane had been their original singer. After she left, there were a number of singers, including Maura O'Connell. Dolores rejoined the group during Mary's stint with them. 'We had a year and a half together in De Danann and we became really close,' Mary recalls. 'It was great having a woman on the road with you. I felt that too about having Máire Breathnach in my band and then Eleanor [McEvoy].'

While it may appear that Mary Black sailed through the various bands without experiencing stormy waters, she dispels this notion. 'Early on in De Danann there was some sorting out to do, territorial rights, just straightening out exactly where we stood with each other. I thought at first it wasn't going to work because there were little things that were bothering me and things that were bothering others. But, before long we had it all sorted out and everyone knew where they stood. It's all about getting to know each other and understanding each other, just like any relationship.' After a successful run with De Danann, Mary finally had to call it a day. 'So much was happening in my solo career and I was having kids through all this. I started to look seriously at getting a band together and working solo.'

The turning point in Mary's solo career came with the release of the album *No Frontiers*. 'I think it stood out as being something special from every point of view, from performance and material to the actual recording. It also brought me to a broader audience. Bill Straw of Gifthorse Records in America got to hear us through the song, "No Frontiers", on a radio programme one day and signed us up for America. We followed up the release of the album with an American tour and got excellent reviews in *Rolling Stone*, *The Washington Post* and *The San Francisco Chronicle*. *No Frontiers* also alerted the attention of Mr Fugimoto of King Records in Japan. He released it in Japan and there was an impressive reaction to it there. That's how the relationship in Japan started. We've been there twice and we are going back again in the New Year.

'Japan is very different. They are just so organised. There is a language barrier and straight away that puts you at a disadvantage. But people can communicate through music regardless of language. Before we left Ireland they asked us to send them a set list – usually we would do it two hours before the show. They made up a beautiful programme of the eighteen songs in English and Japanese, so the audience could understand the words while they were listening to the music. And during the show they became very emotional. When people in Ireland are really enjoying a show they become very verbal and start shouting, yahooing and clapping. But the Japanese start to cry when they are moved. The biggest compliment they can give you is to cry. And that's what happened. When they came backstage afterwards they would hardly look you in the eye because they felt so impressed by what you had just done.

'They are incredibly generous and give presents. They got to know that I had three children and they would come up to the stage and leave little gifts for them. I had to buy a huge bag with wheels on it when I was coming home because of the amount of stuff they gave me. I was very impressed with the Japanese. I thought they were lovely people. They work very hard and they are serious about what they do. But when they unwind and relax they are great fun and I got on very well with them.

'Women in Japan have a tough time. They were intrigued by me being a mother and being able to have a career like this. They couldn't believe that my husband would allow me to work and travel so much abroad. I told them it was quite normal back home. That if women want to work it's not frowned upon – generally speaking, it's very accepted and that's the way it should be, provided the children are properly looked after. In Japan, it's not accepted that they leave their children with anybody other than their family. As soon as they get married, a lot of women there give up their work – certainly if they have a child they have to stop working. Many of them decide not to have children because they are very ambitious. They have a very materialistic way of thinking. Being successful and having a good education and a good job is very important to them. So a lot of them choose not to have children although they would dearly love them. I think that's very sad. And a lot of them don't get married because of that.'

Mary met her husband, Joe O'Reilly, through a mutual love of Gaelic football. 'Our backgrounds are very similar. Joe went to Synge Street Christian Brothers secondary school and my brothers went there also. He played football for Synge Street and I got to know a lot of the players. I used to go to the matches and we met up through that. It had nothing to do with the music. Joe has always been very, very supportive and in the early days he gave me the push that I needed, a good kick in the backside to get out and do it. I was nervous in the early days. I'd worry about what I had to offer and was it that great. And he was the one who would say, "C'mon, you're well able to do it." I'd be delighted when I did it. But there were times when I wanted to turn things down because I was so nervous of doing them. Things like singing solo for half-an-hour at the Meeting Place [Dublin music pub], which I've done.

'Joe has been a real friend with whom I can discuss things and certainly in the last ten years you couldn't fault his management. He has my interests at heart because he's the father of my children. So I haven't had this screaming pressure from a manager who would be pushing me into a lot of work commitments. In this business you have to learn to say No. You could be working all the time. The pressure would build up and things could start to crumble. You have to look at the whole picture.

He has made some very good deals on my behalf and I haven't been ripped off. He has a very good business head. I'm probably one of the very few people that has escaped being ripped off in this business. Everybody in the music business has a story to tell. We haven't gone headlong into things that sound very attractive. That's often where you can make a mistake – somebody tries to impress you by telling you where you're going to be this time next year. We've heard all that. You can't take people at face value. You have to examine everything carefully because you could be signing yourself into a contract for five years and by the time you get out your career could be gone.'

   Mary's parents, Kevin (now deceased) and Patricia Black played a major role in nurturing her love of music as a child and she has fond memories of those early days. 'Oh, they were a huge influence,' she acknowledges. 'Both my father and my mother had a love of music and especially singing, which is probably what we do best, that was readily passed on to us all. My mother, who was a Daly before she married, was a singer. Not a professional singer, but she loved to sing. My father came from a really rural part of Ireland up near the north coast of Antrim – Rathlin Island. He came from a more traditional background and played fiddle and mandolin. He wasn't a brilliant player, but he had the enthusiasm and the love of it.

   'When we were young, every Sunday evening there was a session, or as we used to call it, a hooley, in the house. There'd be music and maybe a few of Dad's friends would come in. I'd do a bit of Irish dancing and we'd all have to sing. This was in the heart of the city. We were in a rough area of Dublin, so it was a bit unusual, although I thought every family was like that when I was a kid. But our parents instilled in us a love and respect for music. I think that's a very important thing to have, regardless of how successful you are. If the main reason for you being involved in it is because you love it and enjoy it, then you're half-way there. They enjoyed any success we had. When we'd come home from a gig, Mother would want to know the details of every little thing that happened. She'd be living every minute of it. They both did. Daddy died three years ago, but did live long enough to see my success and the beginning of Frances's. I'd love him to see Frances's success now. They were both very proud of us and always encouraged us in any way they could and supported us when we weren't working.'

Mary's father left his native Rathlin Island when he was in his early twenties. 'He had to leave the island because there was no work on Rathlin, no way of making a living. It broke his heart to leave Rathlin. Island people are like that, there's nowhere like their birth place. He went off and practised his trade as a plasterer in Cushendal and around that area of County Antrim. He formed a *céilí* band, The Kevin Black Céilí Band, and he used to play at the local dances. Coming from Rathlin, he had never been troubled by the Catholic/Protestant divide. Catholics and Protestants lived on the island in harmony. Everyone went to the socials in the local hall and there would be Protestant tunes and Catholic tunes. Daddy never differentiated between the two in his mind. So when he went away to the mainland he used to play all the music he knew. But there they thought he was trying to stir up trouble. He was working for a Protestant, who was a very nice man. The man came to him one day and said, "I'm going to have to let you go. I've been tipped off by the police. They think you're trying to stir something up. You're playing these rebel tunes. Your name is in all the barracks all around the North of Ireland as being a troublemaker."

'Daddy was the gentlest man alive. He was never into violence in any shape or form and he would never incite anything. He was very upset about it. He packed his bags and said, "I'm going to Dublin." He didn't know anyone in Dublin. He arrived on a train, got on to a No. 20 bus and asked the busman to let him off somewhere where he might find digs. He was left off at Kelly's Corner and pointed towards Charlemont Street, which is where we were all born and reared. It's amazing to think he never left there – and he was in Dublin for fifty years. It was a few years before he met my mother. They met through mutual friends. She was from Dublin. He was a great storyteller. You'd enjoy listening to him. "I remember back in ..." he'd say, and he'd have all the names and all the dates.'

The late Kevin Black ensured that his young children had the best of both worlds. Every summer he would take them out of the city and up to Rathlin Island. He shared his own background with them and he was anxious that they should form a relationship with the land and the people of his birthplace. And when he died he left a house on the island as a holiday home for all his children, so that they could introduce his grandchildren to the beauty and the culture of Rathlin Island. 'My father used to pack us off to Rathlin Island as soon as we got the summer holidays and we'd be up there for six to eight weeks. It was a huge advantage to our development because we were coming from the streets and going up to this place which was the complete opposite. Just wild fields, no electricity and none of the things that we thought were normal. So we were able to weigh the two things and take the best from both worlds. I appreciated it even as a child. I knew we were special when I looked around at my friends in the sense that we had another world to go off to. I used to cry coming back from Rathlin. We existed without electricity – they used candles and oil lamps there. The food was basic. They'd go fishing for mackerel and you'd have fresh eggs and vegetables. We used to love the animals, the cows and the chickens and the sheep. To us, they were amazing. We'd come home incredibly upset. We had a great fondness for it and still do. We are really sentimental and soppy about it to this day.'

Although she's now proud of her origins in Dublin's Charlemont Street, Mary does admit that there was a time when she tried to disown her background. 'When I was in the choir I was mixing with the middle class, people who lived in real houses. Ours was a tenement house. To me, it wasn't an ordinary house. Everyone else's house had a front garden and a back garden. We had a house that led out onto the street and it was in a rough area. It never bothered me living there. It wasn't as if I was a toffee-nosed kid who happened to be living in a rough street. We were street kids. We were rough as well in our own way. It was only when I went to secondary school that it bothered me. I remember getting off the bus and walking past my house. I was a real Judas when asked where I lived. I said: "Up around the corner." But I suppose many kids are like that at a certain stage in their lives. They become ashamed of their parents, ashamed of the fact that their home isn't as nice as everyone else's.

'I was even ashamed of my name! I used to be called "Nigger". Black was a name that didn't sit comfortably beside everyone else's name. When I was very young I used to have a real problem with it. And I remember how one particular nun at school also used to have a problem with it. One day the *cigire* [school inspector] came into the classroom. He was going around with the nun and asking her what everyone's name was. When they came to me the nun said, "Oh, that's Mary Blake." She couldn't even bring herself to say Black. So when she reacted in that way I was really ashamed. And whenever people asked me my name I'd mutter it under my breath. Looking back, it seems the word Black was somehow derogatory!'

Mary told Damien Corless of *In Dublin* magazine that she has been a feminist and still has feminist views at times. 'I still feel that it's a man's world and I say to my boys, "You're lucky that you are male because it's an easier world for a man." But I think it's no longer anything that men are doing to us to make it like that, although there are still countries where that needs to be sorted out – Japan, for instance, is ridiculous. I think women have stood up and fought and gained a lot of respect over the last twenty years, but it's something you must always look out for because it could slip again.' She feels that women's problems are as much biological as social. 'Women have to carry the child around for nine months and then suffer the guilt of being away from their children if they want to work outside the home. Then women have to face the change of life. I've seen friends going through hell and the only change I've seen in men is that they start looking at younger women and worrying about how they look.'

On the question of abortion, Mary says: 'I have a problem with abortion in that I'm against it, yet at the same time I am very sympathetic to women when they say it's their body and it's their right. But I can't justify abortion myself, so I'm glad the abortion referendum went the way it did. And that confuses me because I have all these other feelings that really make me angry about how women are treated, the X-case and all that. It will take a long time to sort it out in my head and the bottom line for me is that I think abortion is wrong under any circumstances, it is taking a life.' She feels that Irish women who decide to have their pregnancy terminated shouldn't be allowed to do it here. 'I feel that if we allow abortion here, that fifteen- and sixteen-year-olds who might find themselves pregnant and considering abortion would see us as endorsing the thing and feel: If it's legal it must be okay. That's the way I feel at the moment, but I could change on that. I try to keep an open mind and I have mixed feelings, but I keep coming back to the question: Is it right or is it wrong? ... and it's wrong.'

Mary, however, readily admits that her husband and manager Joe O'Reilly, has given her the type of support a partner needs in order to be able to pursue other areas outside the home. 'I've had that extra support. If I was a single mother I wouldn't have been able to manage as well. Also, I've got very, very good back-up. I've got somebody who looks after my kids and has done so since they were small and has a good relationship with them. She's part of the family.' There is also the support of the extended family. The Blacks are a close-knit clan. Her mother will step into the breach whenever required. Her sister, Frances, also looks after Mary's children when she's away and vice versa. Mary's husband generally doesn't travel with her, so he's there in the evening and in the morning for their children. Because she has total control over her own career, Mary insists that foreign tours are no longer than three weeks. It's an arrangement that has worked for herself and her family down through the years.

What about her own support for republicanism? 'I now respond to each individual thing as it happens. I no longer slap everything under one umbrella and say, "This is how I feel about the whole thing." I still take the nationalistic view of things in the North. I am sympathetic towards the Catholics. But, on the other hand, nowadays when I think about an RUC man being shot or someone being killed in front of his wife and child, or Enniskillen, I find I react too against that form of cruelty and violence. I lean towards the nationalistic view because it is a natural thing for me to do, but as I grow older I learn to see things also from the other side. I now see all violence and cruelty and bloodshed as wrong. And the tragic part is, I see no solution to the problem.'

Although recognising that the peace movements can do very little to influence the course of events, Mary is full of admiration for the people who took to the streets after the Warrington bomb to protest against the continuing violence. She told Damien Corless: 'Even if the IRA stopped shooting tomorrow, there is no easy solution to what's going on up there. Or if the British Army left the North there would be carnage in the North. Everybody is being hurt by this. Every family in the North. People being shot by soldiers, people in the IRA who've been shot by the other crowd. It's really got out of hand and we need to say Stop! and try to think of the word "peace". But that's not likely to happen.'

The daughter of a Northern Irish Catholic father, Mary Black has heard the litany of injustices and stifled opportunities. 'I know a lot of Catholics who lived up there in the sixties and prior to that, who had a terrible time and who were really second-class citizens,' she told Corless. 'So there are very understandable reasons why that whole thing started. But how it has developed and how it has got out of hand is the problem now. I wonder how the IRA think? Do they really think that if they continue to do what they are doing they'll get what they want? There's a lot of bigotry on both sides. There's a lot of hate, a lot of stuff that will take generations to lose. There's no easy way out because there's always the other side of the argument. Ideally, I'd love to see – I think Ireland should be one country, but I don't think it's even an option.'

Mary sees herself as a 'fairly reasonable person'. In a *Sunday World* interview she said: 'I do get uptight at times and I can be a bit unreasonable, but generally I'm fairly level-headed. I think I'm easy enough to get on with as well. I've never had serious problems getting on with people I work with. I make an effort and I like to think that they make an effort back. I think it's important to have a good working relationship with the people you work with, otherwise I wouldn't enjoy it – it would be the end, so really it's very important for me. I really enjoy what I do. I get a kick out of doing well. I'm not ambitious in such a way that I would do anything to get to the top. I was never ruthlessly ambitious. I think that I have been very lucky with the way that things fell for me – meeting up with Declan [Sinnott, her producer and guitarist], and the way it turned out that Joe ended up being my manager. It wasn't a big plan. It just fell that way and I think I've been very lucky with the things that happened to me in my life. But I look after it and I work hard to keep it going well and keep it from falling apart. It's a business too and there are business problems that crop up from time to time that are worrying. But you'll always come up against things that might upset you and you have to wade your way through. You have to be tough and be able to take criticism. Criticism isn't really pleasant, but you have to take it and bounce back. The best way to answer anybody who might not like what we do is to work harder, do it better and make it more successful.'

When Mary Black sings about heartbreak and longing, one could be forgiven for assuming that she is drawing on personal experience. It's a credit to her skill as an artiste of song that she can evoke such heartfelt and sincere emotions. 'I understand those feelings,' she told Hot Press. 'I especially understand what women can go through. And I do believe that you can understand and feel emotions that have been experienced by people close to you. Maybe not as intrinsically as the person who suffered, but strong enough to interpret songs. I mean, I come from a rough working-class area in town and I've seen a lot of violence. Luckily, not from within my own home.' But Mary has experienced heartbreak in love. 'My heart has been broken badly at least three times because of love and I draw on those experiences for the sad songs. I can relate to feelings women often have of helplessness. Like sometimes I feel so frustrated by not being physically as strong as a man, by being a woman who can't fight back. But relating to the despair other women feel in similar situations and drawing on my frustrations in those areas means I can throw myself right into a song without having been there.'

Women often come up to Mary after a show and say things like, 'That song could have been written for me.' She explains: 'I'm very aware of being honest with people. I don't practise my lines to introduce songs and sometimes it works well and sometimes it doesn't. But at least it's me and how I'm feeling at that moment in time.' A large slice of Mary Black's success is related to her choice of songs. Her latest album, The Holy Ground, features seven songs by Irish songwriters, including Noel Brazil, Paul Doran, Gerry O'Beirne and Thom Moore. She has also covered songs in the past by Irish writers Jimmy McCarthy, Mick Hanly, Donagh Long, Johnny Duhan, Kieran Goss. Mary has so far resisted the temptation to include a self-penned song. 'I feel that so far I haven't written a song that's up to the standard that I'm getting and until I do I won't interfere with what I've got,' she said. 'I feel there are a lot of brilliant songwriters out there who are really glad of a vehicle like myself to put their songs out to the public.' Of her latest album, Mary says: 'I'm really happy with the material, which is a very large part of what we do – to have strong material. I feel there is a lot more energy on this album, which might have been lacking in some of my past albums. It's slightly more "rock" in ways; then there are songs that are the complete opposite to that. It's very much us. But it's two years down the road since *Babes In The Wood*. You're influenced by music you're hearing all the time. I think we are more mature and we have changed. How we feel about what we want to do now is different to how we felt two years ago. Having said that, it's still very much us. But I do feel it's very fresh.'

On a personal level, although she obviously enjoys it, Mary says that she often feels the pressure of coping with the demands of touring. 'It can be tough but it's been mostly good. I try to stay fit when I'm not on the road. I play basketball. I go into the gym whenever I can. I think being active when you're not on the road gives you the energy to cope when you are. I have to look after myself when I'm touring. I can't be partying all night. You have to mind the body and once I do that I seem to be able to keep on top of it. I enjoy a drink, but when I'm touring I have to watch it. When you come off the stage and the adrenalin is really flying, the last thing you want to do is go to bed in a hotel room. But working at that level you have to learn to wind down a bit faster than your body is allowing you to. I find a drink after a show is very good, very therapeutic and it does wind me down, and I allow myself that. The band are very good and we get on very well. We are good friends. We have built up strong relationships over the years and I think everybody supports each other.'

A high-flying showbiz career can take its toll on an artiste's health and appearance, but Mary Black shows no signs of the ravages it can wreak. Yet, she doesn't follow any particular regime as regards diet. 'I watch what I eat, but I'm not silly about it.'

Comparing the high points in her life, she has no hesitation in saying that the best thing that ever happened to her is her three children, Conor (12), Danny (8) and Roisin (5). With her eldest child approaching his teens, Mary admits that the responsibilities of parenthood are even more daunting, particularly in this age of drugs and AIDS. 'When we were teenagers we did try different things,' she told *In Dublin*, 'but I would be worried about Ecstasy and, of course, heroin. I would be worried about the whole speeding up of the heart-rate thing. It's ridiculous just how protective you become of your kids. I'm just like my mother and I used to say: I'll never be like that. I try to talk to them about it. I think it's important to have an open relationship with your kids and for them, hopefully, to be able to talk to you about everything. You become a parent and you are a parent. You worry for them and you don't want them to do that [drugs], you don't want them to do anything like that. My God, you don't even want them to drink!' Reflecting on her own teenage years, she admits: 'Jesus, I used to go out and get locked. But when it comes to your own kids it's just ridiculous how sensible you become. I have to make sure that I don't come over as the big heavy-handed parent because that makes them go the other way. I try to be the understanding, supportive parent.'

She feels that being involved in the music business does tend to keep her young mentally and in tune with young people. 'Definitely. I look around at people of my own age, who maybe were at school with me, and to me they seem older. Maybe they don't look older, but their attitudes are different. I've seen a lot over the years. I've had many experiences on the road and I don't think there's much I don't know about. I sometimes look at my kids and I think they're quite conservative. I was quite innocent up to the age of fifteen or sixteen, then I began to live. But I look at teenagers now in general and they're quite conservative and very sensible – there's a few I know who are much more sensible than we were. It's a very difficult time for them. They're being warned about everything from AIDS to smoking. They know all the dangers whereas we knew nothing. In the old days the fear was that you'd get pregnant – now you're looking at a death sentence. I really do feel sorry for young kids now.'

Talking about the success of *A Woman's Heart* album she says: 'Joe and his brother Paul O'Reilly from Dolphin were putting together a compilation of Irish music from their own catalogue. The idea developed into an album of exclusively female Irish artistes. I had been listening to Eleanor McEvoy's songs – she was in my band then – and suggested that she record a couple of her songs for the album. Though Eleanor was relatively unknown at the time I thought it would be a good idea to introduce a new artiste alongside established artistes on the compilation. We both went in and recorded the song "Only A Woman's Heart", which, in my opinion, played a major part in the success of the album.

'All the artistes involved benefited greatly from the *Woman's Heart* album, particularly Eleanor and my sister Frances. I feel it brought them very quickly to a much wider audience.'

Why is it such a massive success? 'Number one, I think it's a very good compilation. If you sit down and listen to it from beginning to end you'll find that it's not just songs that were thrown together. A bit of thought went into it, even the running order – how one track runs into the next – which to a lot of people might not seem important, but it is. It also has a very varied selection of stuff which I feel is pleasing. Also, I think the title track was very strong. It was the main track that was played, and the support the radio stations gave it was fantastic. And with Eleanor being a new emerging talent it was exciting.' There were no ego clashes between any of the women on the album. 'We are actually all very good friends. We all get on very well. And it's a genuine friendship. I'm an old friend of Dolores from way back, from De Danann days. We keep in touch all the time. Frances, my sister, and I always got on. And Eleanor worked with me for a year and a half and we became really close. Maura and myself go back a long way too because she had De Danann associations. We also kept in touch. Sharon (Shannon) is probably the one I knew least.'

On coping with her status as a household name and singing star, Mary says: 'I don't really think about it very much.' Has she ever stood back and contemplated her position? 'Now and again. When you walk into a place like the Point Theatre in Dublin and there are seven thousand people there, all coming to hear you, you ask yourself: Why are they all so excited? It's a great feeling to play to an enthusiastic audience. And having such talented musicians with you makes for a very exciting live show. I feel the current line-up is the best we've ever had. With Declan on guitars, Pat Crowley on piano and accordion, Garvan Gallagher on bass, Carl Geraghty on saxophone, Dave Early on drums and percussion, and Frank Gallagher on fiddle, synths and whistle.'

She told *In Dublin* that success has given her: 'A nice house. A little cottage in the country. Things we would otherwise have been a lot longer trying to get together, but the main thing that it hasn't done is ruin anything. Not that I have an awful lot, but I'm comfortable. I feel really privileged that I have a good home life and three lovely kids and have loads of that love that so many people in the music business lack or lose out on. In this

business generally the amount of broken marriages is unbelievable. It's a selfish life in ways because you're always going off
and someone is left behind and that's never easy. I've managed
to keep things balanced and I've got the good things out of the
music business and left the nasty stuff behind – hopefully. We're
older now and the quality of life becomes more important. With
that too goes the fact that we need to enjoy what we're doing.
If it becomes a chore for me, if I don't enjoy two or three gigs
in a row, I start to worry and I decide: If this continues I'm going
to stop, I'm not doing it. I've never been bitten by any huge
ambition to be famous, or rich, I'm just doing what I enjoy
doing. And I'm getting paid for it.' Having achieved so much in
her career, is there anything else that would give her a buzz? 'I
wouldn't mind getting a Grammy. But there are a few ideas I'd
like to pursue which I know I would really find exciting. Sure,
life's a buzz!'

ABOVE: The Black family. *Left to right*, Martin, Mary (aged 10), Michael (*behind*), Frances (aged 5), Uncle John (*behind*), cousin Brenda.
BELOW: Frances (*left*) and Mary Black with their mother.

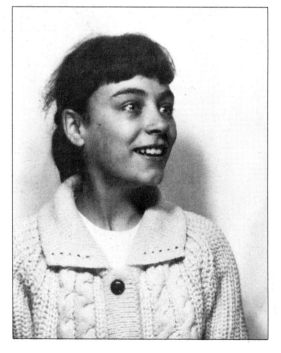

ABOVE LEFT: Schoolgirl, Mary Black.
LEFT: Mary as a teenager.
ABOVE: Mary on her First
Communion day.

SINGER, MARY BLACK

LEFT: Mary Black in concert.
ABOVE: Frances and Mary Black with promoter Pat Egan.
BELOW: Mary and Frances singing with The Black Family.

SISTERS MARY AND FRANCES BLACK

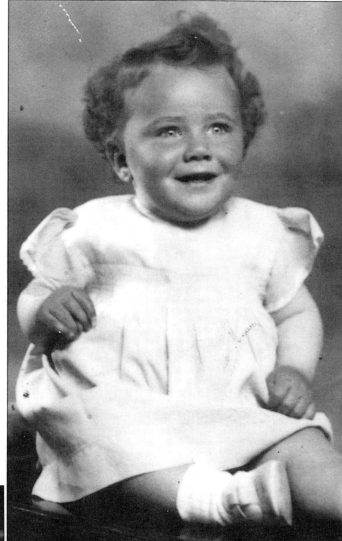

RIGHT: Frances Black on her first birthday.
BELOW, LEFT: Frances with her daughter Aoife on holidays, 1989.
BELOW, RIGHT: Frances with her son Eoghan and Sharon Shannon, 1988.

ABOVE: Frances Black singing at a Gateaux workers' rally, 1990.
BELOW: Frances with the group Arcady.

ABOVE: Frances Black on the Aran Islands with Kieran Goss (*left*) and James Blennerhasset, 1992.
BELOW: Frances, with Kieran Goss.

ELEANOR McEVOY

TOP, LEFT: Baby Eleanor McEvoy. TOP, RIGHT: Eleanor on her First Communion day. ABOVE: Graduation day, Trinity College – Eleanor McEvoy (*second from right, back row*).

ABOVE: Eleanor McEvoy with her brother Kieran. BELOW: Eleanor McEvoy.

ELEANOR McEVOY

ELEANOR McEVOY

OVE, LEFT: Dolores Keane (*right*) with her sister Christina. ABOVE, RIGHT: Dolores with her father, g Matt. BELOW: A session at the Keane house. *In front*, Dolores, playing the tin whistle; *at the back*, ristina; *left to right*, Paddy (uncle), Mary (aunt), Rita and Sarah (aunts), Tom (uncle).

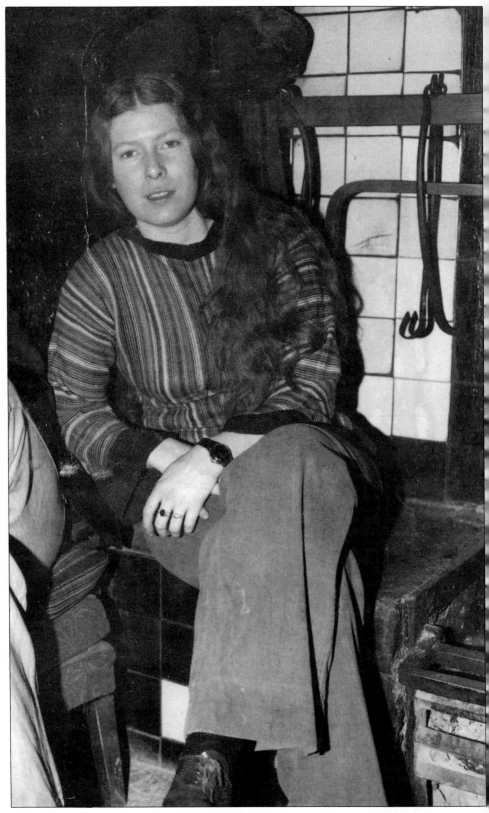

A YOUNG DOLORES KEANE

ABOVE, LEFT: Dolores Keane.
ABOVE, RIGHT: Dolores Keane with musician Jackie Small.
LEFT: Dolores (*front, right*) with her grandmother, and (*behind*) Aunt Sarah and Uncle Tom.

DOLORES KEANE

FRANCES BLACK

FRANCES BLACK

Frances Black vividly recalls her first public performance – with two musicians who had invited her to become their lead singer. Like any nightmare experience, it's etched on her memory for eternity. And it's a real life story that will serve to give encouragement to young singers hoping to pursue a career in the music business, because it demonstrates how even the most gifted singers often have to get to grips with a lack of confidence or stage fright during their initial tentative steps into the public arena.

'I was about fifteen or sixteen and it was a time when Mary [Black, her sister] was really starting to make a name for herself,' Frances recalls in a special interview for this book. 'Two fellas in the music scene, who were session players, were looking for a singer. One played the guitar and the other played the *bodhrán* and they had heard that Mary Black had a sister who could sing. So they contacted me and I said, "Yeah, OK, sure it'll be a bit of *craic*." So I rehearsed a number of songs with them; English folk songs like "The Blackleg Miner" and songs like "Ramblin' Irishman" and "Eighteen Years Old". Eventually the night arrived and we got up on stage in the venue, Slattery's of Capel Street in Dublin. Your man on the guitar gave me the note and – nothing. I couldn't get anything out. I just couldn't sing. And when words eventually came after an embarrassing struggle they were gobbledegook. I froze and I said to the audience, "I can't do it." Then I walked off the stage.

'The audience all clapped to give me a bit of support and I

was mortified. I came down off the stage and sat in a corner while the lads played on, and I didn't know whether to cry or throw up or both. After the show the lads came over to me and said, "It doesn't matter. It doesn't matter." And they wanted to pay me. They got about thirty pounds for the night and they were giving me a fiver. They still had this dream in their heads of having me as a singer. But that was the end as far as I was concerned. I swore, "Never again." It was such a nightmare. A really humiliating experience.'

Despite this traumatic start to her career, Frances overcame her stage fright and a couple of years later she joined her sister, Mary and brothers, Shay, Michael and Martin, in the The Black Family. Apart from their spine-tingling five-part harmonies, the individual members of the group also took their turn in the spotlight to do solo performances and Frances soon learned to savour the experience. 'It was much easier with The Black Family because they did all the singing and I just sang one solo song. And they were behind me all the time saying, "Go on, you can do it." They were rooting for me, so it was much easier. I don't think I could have done it only for that. I don't think I could have got up and sung on my own with a strange band.' She describes how devastated she was when they went off on an American tour and left her behind. 'I was in school at the time and I wasn't allowed to go. I was raging. But when they came back and decided to do a tour of the folk clubs around Ireland I put my foot down and said: "I can sing too." So I did that tour and it was great craic. We did two major tours of Ireland in the mid-eighties.'

Frances points to the eldest of the family, Shay Black, as the one responsible for leading her into music. 'Shay was the one who started us all off. He was mad into music. He saved up and bought himself a guitar at the age of twelve. He was really dedicated and he listened to all the music. He listened to the Beatles. Then he listened to folk music. It was around the time that Planxty and all those groups were coming on the scene. We weren't all music listeners at the time. But my mother would sing and my father would sing when people called. We always had a radio in the house and listened to the music on that. It was Shay who went out and bought himself a stereo and started to listen to all types of music. Then he taught himself how to play the guitar. He got Michael interested in music. Michael went off and bought himself a banjo. He was mad keen to play when he saw Shay doing really well. Michael became a brilliant banjo player. It was around the time of the Dubliners and he really admired Barney McKenna. He was the business. Mary always sang. Even when she was in the choir she was a soloist. Shay started to get Mary to learn songs and he would accompany her. Martin also picked up the fiddle and guitar and, of course, he was always a great singer.'

Although she has now established herself as a major force on the Irish music scene, Frances Black has fought a tremendous personal battle to achieve her current status. As a young adult it seemed that the odds were suddenly stacked up heavily against her ever making a success of her life. She became pregnant at nineteen, married and had a second child, all within two years. The pressure of married life, motherhood and financial difficulties eventually became too great to handle. Frances developed a drink problem and her marriage broke up. It was a nightmare beginning to her adult life. It was not how she dreamt her world would be as a carefree street kid growing up in the tough but close-knit community in Dublin. 'Charlemont Street was a great area to be brought up in,' Frances says, looking back on her early days. 'There was always a great community spirit. My mother had a shop there and we were all known. I used to hang around the flats because that's where all my pals were. We had great *craic*. We played all the games like Relieveo, where you chased people and put them into a den. But football was the main thing and, of course, fancying the fellas when you came to the age of twelve or thirteen.

'When I was about ten or eleven, Shay said, "Frances, it's time for you to start singing". He sat me down and taught me my first song, "Donna, Donna, Donna" and he backed me with his guitar. When the *seisiúns* started at home I began to learn other songs and we'd all sing in harmony together.

'I hated school. I went into a transition year after doing my Inter Cert., which I passed with two honours. The transition year was an experimental thing. Then I went to Rathmines Tech. But I just wasn't a very responsible person. I liked to have the *craic*. So I left school in the middle of fifth year. I minded kids for a while and then I went to America with my brother, Michael. We were based in Connecticut. I was an *au pair* for a family. Michael was working for the husband, who was a builder. I wanted to go to America to see what it was like. I thought it would be real glamorous, but it wasn't at all. I was minding four kids and I had no experience. I was thrown in at the deep end. I was running the whole house because the wife had gone to Ireland to write a book. So, home to me Mammy I thought I'd never get! We were in America for three months, but in the last month we toured around the east coast. When I came home I worked part-time as a waitress in the Harcourt Hotel. Then I got pregnant, so that was the end of that. I was nineteen.'

Frances and her boyfriend, Richard, married after their son, Eoghan, was born. A year later she gave birth to a daughter, Aoife. 'We were both very young and it was tough. We were too young, really. I went from being a very irresponsible person to being a responsible person and it was a bit of a shock for me. The first year I had Eoghan I also looked after another kid of the same age. That was very difficult as well because they were two babies. I was twenty, but I was an immature twenty. I hadn't a clue. I didn't go out very much during the day. When Richard came home in the evening he'd do all the shopping. We were living in a rented house in Ranelagh at the time. We lived there for the first year.

'But the second year, when I was having Aoife, we moved to my mother's home because the rent was too expensive. We stayed there for a time and then we moved into the Corporation flats across the road. I never went outside the door with the two kids. There were lots of stairs to negotiate in the flats, so I didn't bother going out. The kids would be having their sleeps, so I just got into a routine of staying in. Then I got a job, which was great because I had no confidence in myself. I was a very shy, really introverted person. With the job I was out meeting people again. But I found it very difficult initially. I was working in a coffee bar at Ricardo's Snooker Hall in Camden Street. It was brilliant and I made great friends and it gave me a bit of confidence.

'In 1985, Richard and myself split up. We just couldn't cope with the pressures of married life, financial problems, the whole thing. I had met Richard when I was sixteen or seventeen and after being together for eight years I found the break-up to be very traumatic, particularly as there were kids involved. You have to be very strong for the kids and after the break-up I became a very strong person. After that, I felt I could take on the world. But the loneliness was hard to deal with initially. There were lots of things that led to the break-up. I was drinking at the time. Being immature. Not being able to cope with the adult problems of it all. Neither of us could cope with it. We both blamed each other. It's a very easy thing to do. So I think it was inevitable that we would split up. We are great friends now. He comes up twice or three times a week to see the kids. We get on better now than we ever did. And he's very happy now in another relationship. After the split, two very good friends, Nuala and Brid, took me in and looked after me. I could never really repay them for what they did. They took me into their home with the two kids. I stayed with them for a while and then I moved back into Charlemont Street where my brother Martin was now living. And then Martin minded me for a while. I lived there for a year.

'At this stage I was asked to join Arcady. Initially, I was petrified. It was a big decision to make. But I couldn't turn it down either because of the people who were going to be involved in it. As far as I was concerned, Johnny McDonagh was a megastar because he had been in De Danann for so many years. The other members were all very well known musicians on the traditional music scene: Brendan Larrissey, Patsy Broderick, Seán Keane, Cathal Hayden, Sharon Shannon and Paul Doyle. I was really, really honoured to be asked to join them. They asked me through Mary. Johnny met Mary and asked Mary. I was really taken aback and shocked by the offer. Then Johnny came to a Black Family gig in Galway and he came backstage and asked me himself. I said Yes. So I joined Arcady and that was a huge stepping stone in my life. I'm not just talking about my singing career. I'm talking about my personal development.

'Just before I joined Arcady in 1988, I had given up drinking. Drink had become a problem. I was an alcoholic. Not a raving alcoholic, but I was an alcoholic. My problem with drinking was that I'd have to have a few pints every night in order to sleep. Even when I was at home I'd have a few cans of beer or I'd have wine. Some kind of drink. I just loved it. And once I started there was no stopping me. But I didn't think it was affecting my life that much. I felt there was something wrong and I wanted to give it up, but I couldn't. Then I read a newspaper report about a support group in Stanhope Street. There was a story about one particular woman who said she used to drink a bottle of wine every evening when she came home from work. So I thought maybe I have a problem because sometimes I'd drink more than a bottle. Sometimes I'd drink two bottles of wine a night.

'I rang them up and I said, "I don't really have a problem, but I want to give up drink." So I went down to see a counsellor and I was asked a list of questions and at the end of it I said, "Now, I don't have a drink problem but I just want to give up drink. Can you help me?" She said to me, "Frances, there is no doubt in my mind, you are an alcoholic." Well, I cycled home in a state of shock. Initially I was thinking, Ah, she doesn't know what she's talking about. But I did the course and it was an amazing course. They teach you an awful lot about life as well and about people in general. It educated me about drink. An awful lot of people in Ireland are addicted to it and they don't realise it because they don't reach out for a whiskey or whatever first thing in the morning. Everybody's interpretation of an alcoholic is a wino and somebody who is in the gutter. But that's not the case at all.

'When I joined Arcady, Johnny McDonagh was very supportive and I learned an awful lot just being in the band, apart from the fact that we travelled all over the world. I had never done that much with my life up to then, career-wise. They taught me an awful lot about dealing with people, especially Patsy Broderick with whom I became very close. We still see each other all the time. In the beginning, every time I got up on stage I was absolutely petrified. I couldn't talk to the audience and I couldn't introduce the songs. I used to stutter a lot and stumble and make a fool of myself. But they were all very supportive in the band. They never slagged me. And it all just came with experience eventually. I really owe them a debt of gratitude for believing in me from day one, because I didn't think I could do it. But Johnny did. So I owe Johnny McDonagh an awful lot. When I joined Arcady I had to learn a new set of songs that suited the group. Initially, Johnny wanted to have traditional songs combined with American country. So I learned the country songs, but I wasn't that happy singing them. I'm not a country singer. But I sang them for a while. But when we did an album and single we called them *After The Ball*, and that song was our big hit. P.J. Curtis, who produced the album, selected that song.

'We toured all over the world – Europe, America, Canada, Australia and even Iraq. We performed at a week-long world music festival in Baghdad a year before the Gulf War. We were brought out by the Iraqi government, by head-the-ball himself, Saddam Hussein. You could sense that there was a lot of tension there. All the artistes stayed in a big posh hotel and each country had their own guide. You couldn't go outside your hotel without your guide. At the time, I didn't know who Saddam Hussein was. But they brought us around and they showed us his whole life from the time he was born. And everywhere you went the buildings had big murals of him on the walls. He was like a god. The first gig we did was in a temple in Babylon and we were singing to Iraqi people. But they loved the music. They went mad for it.

'The album was very successful. It went to number six in the Irish charts. And the single, "After the Ball", was number seven. It was also the first time that I got attention from the media and I was chuffed. The album also did really well on the folk scene in America. Arcady were beginning to pull in huge crowds. That's where they had the biggest impact. In Ireland at the time, people weren't that interested in traditional music. It just wasn't the right time, but it's coming back again. It was really happening for the band in America and they wanted to do longer tours there. But it used to break my heart having to leave the kids for three weeks at a time. It was a long time to be away from them. And every time I did it I'd say, "This is the last time. I'm not doing this anymore." Eventually, because Arcady were doing more tours of the States and other countries, I couldn't hack it. I just couldn't commit myself to that amount of travelling. That's when I said it was time to stop. In January 1992, I told them I was leaving. And I left after an American tour the following August. I was very sad leaving them because it had been a great stage of my life and I had developed so much. But we parted on great terms and I still see them a lot. When I left Arcady I never imagined in my wildest dreams that down the road my solo career would suddenly take off in such a big way.'

Despite the fact that she has followed in the footsteps of Mary, who has achieved royal status in her field of music on the Irish scene, Frances maintains that she has never been conscious of living in the shadow of her big sister. Nor has she found that Mary's success has been a hindrance to the advancement of her own career. 'Mary's success was never a problem,' she says. 'It's just that in the early stages I didn't think I could stand out as an artiste in my own right. I didn't think I would ever be capable of it. But that was nothing to do with Mary. It has never really bothered me being Mary Black's sister, even though years ago people would introduce me to other people, saying: "This is Mary Black's sister." Full stop. No first name. I don't think people meant to do it intentionally and they don't mean to hurt your feelings or try to take away your identity. In fact, some people still call me Mary. In the shop the other day a young girl said in her best Dublin accent, "How'ya, Mary?" But I never take offence. And Mary tells me that everywhere she goes now people are talking about me. It's just that kind of business. Mary has been an unbelievable influence on my singing career. She taught me probably everything I know about singing. And she always phones me after a gig to see how it went. Mary and myself are very close. We look after each other's kids whenever one of us has to go away on tour. We're mates. In the beginning, my only concern was that people would think I was trying to cash in on her success. I'd die if I thought people felt that way about me.'

During her time performing with the family group, even before she joined Arcady, Dublin-based promoter and showbiz agent Pat Egan recognised her talent and encouraged Frances to embark on a solo career. 'After he saw The Black Family in the Olympia Theatre in Dublin he used to say to me, "Y'know, Frances, I think you should start doing your own gigs." At the time he owned a Dublin venue called the Backstage Bar, now Bad Bob's, and he gave me a Thursday night residency there for three months. It really built up my confidence because you have to work to get your experience. He always had a belief in me and he wanted to be my agent, but at that time I wasn't ready to go out on my own.'

After the hectic schedule with Arcady, Frances decided to confine her public appearances to occasional performances. 'All I wanted to do was sing and I wanted to gig. I didn't want to give up singing. Once you get up there and sing on stage it never leaves you. You have to get the hit. I just wanted to cut down on the travelling so that I could spend more time with my kids. That was the reason I left Arcady in the first place.' But Frances didn't envisage the success and public demand that would result from her later collaboration with songwriter and musician Kieran Goss from Newry, County Down.

Her brother, Shay, is an avid collector of songs and long before Frances's and Kieran's paths crossed, she was learning a song called 'All That You Ask Me'. The first time Frances saw Kieran Goss in performance, he was singing that particular song. 'I had found the song in Shay's songbook and thought the words in it were great, so I started to learn it. After Kieran's gig I went up to him and said, "That's amazing, you're after singing a song I'm learning." He said, "That's my song." We had already met when I was with Arcady and Kieran was doing solo gigs. But that was the first time we had talked.' Later, Frances was offered some dates in Northern Ireland and she asked Kieran to support her on guitar. 'It worked really well and we got on really well. We had great *craic*,' she recalls.

It started out as a laid-back partnership, with the two performers adoping a casual, fun approach to their shows. But when

Mary asked them to support her in concert, their attitude changed. 'Doing support to Mary, we had to take it a bit more seriously,' Frances explains. 'When you're doing a concert at Dublin's National Stadium and the Ulster Hall in Belfast, it's a totally different scene. We looked for songs and deliberately worked out arrangements to the point where we both saw that it was working really well and it could go somewhere. Then it snowballed after the success of the *Woman's Heart* album.'

Her professional relationship with Kieran Goss has seen Frances Black realise a number of personal ambitions. Her dream of having her name up in lights at Dublin's Olympia Theatre became a reality in May 1993. 'Playing the Olympia Theatre was the ultimate dream,' she enthuses. 'It was the most amazing gig. The audience were absolutely overwhelming in their support. I was nearly crying because it was such an emotional experience when I walked out on stage and they went wild. They clapped and cheered and roared for what seemed like five minutes. I was really taken aback. I really got emotional. If I had hand-picked them, I couldn't have picked a better audience. No matter what you did or what you said they were just into it. I floated home and floated around for a week afterwards. I didn't care if I never did anything again. And I kind of lost interest for a while.

'But then the *Woman's Heart* tour came up and we were back working flat out to huge audiences everywhere we went. It's a real exciting time for us because it's all growing and growing. I love going out on stage when there's a full house. And I love the audience. I love them for coming. It really gives me a thrill. I get an unbelievable buzz out of it. I hate to think I would ever take that for granted. I don't think we ever will. I remember walking out on stage in Mother Red Cap's in Dublin after we had done the first *Woman's Heart* tour and they were hanging out of the rafters. There had been queues down the road before the show and when the doors opened they all charged in. By the time we got to the stage they were waiting for us and were really into us. I got such a kick out of that gig. I remember how I didn't really sing that well, but it didn't matter because they were into us anyway.'

Although a major artiste in her own right nowadays, Frances still gets endearingly starstruck by her peers. She was overawed on a tour of Australia when she found herself travelling and performing in the company of artistes she had idolised. 'From the time I started to go out, I wanted to go and see Moving Hearts, Christy Moore, Donal Lunny and Stockton's Wing. It struck me on the first night of the Australian tour when we all went on stage for the finale. I looked around and I thought: This is weird. There I was in the company of all these people I had admired. I looked around and I said to myself: This is brilliant. It was a real privilege to be working with all the people on the tour. Of course, it was great to see Australia as well. One night we had a *seisiún* in a pub in Sydney with Christy Moore, Donal Lunny, Davy Spillane, Nollaig Casey, all the lads out of Stockton's Wing, Barleycorn and Brendan Grace. There was Christy singing all his songs and Donal playing away and Davy Spillane playing the pipes – it was an incredible experience.'

Featuring on the album, *A Woman's Heart* moved Frances and Kieran into the First Division of the Irish music scene. 'We would never have got to this stage as fast if it hadn't been for the *Woman's Heart* album,' Frances admits. 'I think it was an unusual venture on the record company's part. They brought six women together. It was never done by women before in Ireland. Women were always kept down a bit and the fact that all of a sudden there were six on an album together was unbelievable. I'd imagine the majority of people who bought the album were women. I don't think there was a serious feminist vibe off it. I just think that women are starting to support each other a bit more. Most of the songs on the album, like "Wall of Tears" and "A Woman's Heart", are about lost love.

And a lot of the songs are about men and that is a major feature of the album.'

Frances is now regarded by some women as a person to confide in. 'There was a woman who came up to me after a concert. She sat down beside me and said, "I relate to your songs so much", and she talked to me as if we had known each other all our lives, as if I was her best friend. She told me all her problems. She told me all about her relationship. She was really going through the mill. She really related to me because of my music and because of what she got off the songs. I was chuffed that she felt she could confide in me and pour out her heart to me. The songs on the album were chosen very carefully and I think that's why so many women relate to them and have made it such a success.'

Kieran feels that the album 'tapped into the whole mood of the time. It was a good album and it was in the right place at the right time. It had a life of its own. It had a good fresh sound and it was different and new. You couldn't put a label on the kind of music that was on it. It was a fresh Irish woman's album. It fitted into the overall social changes with Mary Robinson becoming President and women being so much more aware of themselves. I felt that the whole Irish scene was ready for something new and big. Every couple of years a country needs a new big thing. If you are lucky to hit on that, which the *Woman's Heart* album did, then you are it. It's your time. It became one of the albums that you had to have in your collection. There are people I know who have that album who just don't buy albums.' Frances immediately noticed the change in their audiences after the success of the album. 'It's a very mixed audience, ranging from the age of fifteen to seventy.'

Working with Kieran Goss and James Blennerhasset, the third member of the group, has given Frances Black the opportunity to establish a stronger rapport with her audience and to expand her stage presentation, compared to her period with the traditional group Arcady. 'There is a big difference,' she told Siobhán Long in *Hot Press*. 'I enjoyed Arcady a lot. I enjoyed the tours and the *craic*. But in the actual songs I was very limited to a certain number of songs, about eight songs which are the songs on the Arcady album. Now I can do anything and everything I want and it allows us to have this intimate thing with the audience. When I was singing with Arcady, I'd get up and sing and sit down for two or three tunes, which is fifteen minutes, so you can't really get into the whole thing with the audience. When it's just the two of us you can really clutch them in the palm of your hand.' Many people who go along to hear the group for the first time are surprised by the amount of humour in their show and Kieran has won a large following for his witticisms. 'We like to leave the audience with a smile,' he told *The Sunday World*. 'The day of just playing your music and not communicating with the audience, being a musical snob, is a very old fashioned thing. It's an old seventies thing where the more aloof you were the bigger you were. Well, that sort of thing is gone. I think an audience want to know something about an artiste or act. We have the *craic* on stage. We get up and enjoy ourselves and the audience gets the good vibe off us.' James Blennerhasset, a Sligo musician who plays double bass and has performed with Van Morrison and Christie Hennessy, also contributes to the sense of fun. 'James plays a major role in the group. He has a great sense of humour and he's a top-class musician with great charisma,' says Frances.

But there is a more serious side to Frances Black. She's a woman who has strong feelings on various social issues and political injustices. One of the songs on their album is a Christy Moore/Donal Lunny number, 'The Time Has Come', which was written at the time of the H-Block hunger strikes and concerns Patsy O'Hara and the relationship he had with his mother as he was dying. 'I really got emotionally involved in the whole campaign,' Frances told *Hot Press*. 'When I was over in America I met Patsy O'Hara's sister who told me about the song. I just think it's the saddest song I've ever heard in my life. When I sang it the first few times I nearly burst into tears. I think it's one of the finest songs Christy Moore has ever written. Having kids myself and having that kind of bond, I just felt to see her son die must have been a total heartbreak. I don't know how she handled it.'

And in an interview for this book, Frances adds: 'I could never understand how one woman [Margaret Thatcher] who was leading a country could cause so much pain to other women. I could never understand how, as a mother herself, she could let those men die the way she did. I am politically aware and have been involved in different campaigns, generally ones where I feel an injustice has been done. I started off with the anti-nuclear campaign here in Dublin when I was seventeen and the H-Block campaign when I was nineteen. And then the Guildford Four and the Birmingham Six. I really got stuck in – doing gigs for them. It was just myself and my brother Martin, who felt the same way as I do. I would be very politically aware of everything that goes on here in Ireland. I've always sworn that if I ever made a name for myself I'd work for women. Every time I go through Rathmines and I pass the Women's Refuge, I think to myself, I'd love to do something more to help their situation. The Women's Refuge gets nothing. Myself and Eilis Moore were invited up to sing there when Mary Robinson visited it. The Eastern Health Board hired in plants, painted up the place beforehand because it was in bits and as soon as she left they started to take out the plants! And it's really overcrowded. The waiting list is months long. It's ridiculous. I just think that it's terrible that women have to wait to get away from men who beat them up. I feel they really need money badly and there should be some sort of campaign.'

Frances believes that women's rights are in a sorry state in this country. 'I think Irish women don't have very much of a say at all over their own lives, over their own bodies. The majority of the people who are making the laws are men and I think: Who the hell do they think they are, deciding what women should do with their lives? I would love if women in Ireland stuck together more. I'd love if they had more unity and fought for one another. There has been a rape case widely reported in the papers which was really sad. The guy walked out of the court after he admitted to rape. The girl has to live with that for the rest of her life. The guy pleaded guilty. I don't think that should have happened when the guy pleaded guilty. Then there was the Kilkenny incest case. Your man got six years for what he did. It's the pits. Sometimes I think it's going backwards for women.

'I think women are probably improving their own lives. They are coming to the fore and saying: It's time we got a bit of notice. It's time we got a bit of the action. I think women in Ireland are becoming more positive in what they are doing in their lives. They are starting to make careers for themselves. They are starting to look at themselves and starting to be independent. But I don't think the Government is doing anything to make it easier for them. It should be there in the educational system. It should be taught in the schools that we are all equal, men and women.' As a woman who has been through the trauma of a marriage breakdown, Frances feels that divorce should be available in this country. 'I personally would like to be free,' she says. 'I feel people should have that right.'

Frances says that on stage she doesn't preach or try to shove her politics down people's throats. 'But I am a political person and I feel that when you're on stage you should show a bit of what you are,' she says. 'I just do one or two songs that have political or social comment. But I'm not a real militant or anything like that. I just feel very strongly about certain things. Kieran is not particularly a political person and he doesn't bring politics into his music. But I would never do anything on stage to offend anybody.' She is opposed to Section 31 of the Broadcasting Act which prohibits interviews with the likes of Sinn Féin. 'I think that [Section 31] is ridiculous. There are some similarities with South Africa. I remember watching Richard Attenborough on *The Late Late Show* one night. He had been to South Africa to do a film and he was telling Gay Byrne how the people involved in the ANC there "are not allowed to speak on television". People in the audience were aghast. But it's no different here.' Frances is not a member of any political party. 'I always vote for an Independent. I love Tony Gregory. I think he's great. I wish I was in his constituency so that I could vote for him. He's dealing with the people and I feel he understands what they are about. I think he has got good, strong socialist politics.'

In her personal life, Frances is now happy in a relationship with Brian, who is also her manager. Both Mary and Frances are managed by their respective partners. 'It means we have much more control over what we do,' Frances points out. 'I wouldn't have a manager who would be telling me what to do because my family has to take priority over my career. It's great that Brian and Kieran and myself can sit down and make our own plans and decisions. But because we have suddenly become so successful, it's getting to the point where it's becoming scary. The success just doesn't seem to be stopping. It's getting bigger and bigger. Offers are coming in which, in a way, you feel you can't really turn down. But if you do take them on, what will they want from you and does it go beyond stuff you can control? That's something we have to face in the future. But, on the other hand, this year for me has probably been the best year of my life.'

ELEANOR McEVOY

ELEANOR McEVOY

Sitting in a recording studio in Los Angeles, listening to her emotions pouring out from her songs as they were played back, Eleanor McEvoy was suddenly struck with the realisation that she was about to let down the barricades and expose her private life and inner feelings to the world. It was during 1993 – a year that has seen her take her first major step towards an international career by launching her debut album, *Eleanor McEvoy*, through the high-powered American record company, Geffen. The collection is mainly autobiographical, and some of the songs cover her often painful experiences in love. And on that particular day in Los Angeles, surrounded by strangers in the recording studio, panic set in as Eleanor listened to the lyrics. 'I suddenly thought: Am I mad? People are going to know all these very personal things about me. I ran from the room. I'm a fairly private person. I wouldn't turn around to someone and tell them personal things unless I knew them a hell of a long time. And there I was singing:

> *With your lips next to my lips*
> *The night would be so much easier*
> *The day not as hard to face*
> *With you inside this empty space*
> *And with your skin next to my skin*
> *The night ahead could be beautiful*
> *Your body I recall made music of it all*
> *Yes, your body I recall*
> *Made music of it all.*   ('MUSIC OF IT ALL')

But the Dublin singer and songwriter overcame her moment of self-doubt and embarrassment and forged ahead with her album. 'What could I do?' she asks. 'It's my gig [work] and I have to be honest in my songs. I don't like it a lot of the time. But I'm incapable of writing a song and not being honest. It just doesn't work any other way for me. It has to be an honest appraisal of how I feel because the music is coming out of my emotions and the words have to match so that it all fits together.'

Music to Eleanor is, to quote one of her songs, 'as potent as wine'. It's her very life blood. A precocious child, she was first turned on to music at the age of four when she began tinkling with the piano in her home. Her sister Marian, who is also a musician, gave Eleanor her early lessons on the piano. But around the age of seven she took a shine to the saxophone after spotting it being played on the television. From that moment on, she wanted a sax. 'I loved the sound of it. I loved the look of it. I loved the people who played it. I loved everything about it. I was really into it.' Eleanor has often told the story of how her mother was totally opposed to her young daughter becoming a saxophonist. 'Nice girls don't play the saxophone. Nice girls play the violin,' her mother would say. When Christmas came around, Eleanor decided it was her opportunity finally to have her way. A visit to Santa Claus seemed to be the answer. On the way out, her mother wanted to know whether she had asked for a violin. She lied, saying she had. When Christmas morning came around, the present under the tree didn't look remotely like a saxophone. The unwrapping confirmed her fear – it was a violin. Mother had obviously intervened with Santa.

Initially, Eleanor had a love-hate relationship with the violin and even admitted to throwing it across the room in a fit of rage once. 'I wasn't very pleased with it. But then I began to play it and started to teach myself. Then my sister decided I should have proper piano lessons. Not that she wasn't a good teacher, but it's better to have someone outside the family teaching you.

So she got me piano lessons and the girl who was teaching me said I had a good ear and I should be playing the violin. So they sent me for violin lessons then. But by that stage I had every bad habit playing the violin that you can have. I had to unlearn everything I had taught myself and start from scratch again. Learn how to hold the bow. Learn how to hold the violin. Go over all that again. So that was doubly frustrating to an eight-year-old. A damn stubborn eight-year-old.'

Apart from a brief flirtation with becoming an astronaut, Eleanor knew from an early age that she wanted to make music her life. After completing her Leaving Certificate examination at Stanhope Street Secondary School, Eleanor joined 'little orchestras' in the College of Music and played with the National Youth Orchestra before moving on to Trinity College to pursue a degree in music. 'So all of a sudden, I'm in Trinity doing music with a group of people who are as crazy about music as I am. I thought I'd died and gone to heaven. It was wonderful. I spent all day talking about music. Analysing music. Listening to music. In that course, you don't play music. It's completely academic. They wanted you to write fugues and piano sonatas and to say why Mozart did this here or that there. I found it all fascinating.'

Eleanor stresses that she was by no means a pampered rich kid whose dreams were being indulged by doting parents. 'Not all students in Trinity are rich. Some of them are. But not all of them.' Eleanor fell into the latter category, so by night she used her musical talent to earn a living. She also taught violin for cash. 'I was very lucky to be able to support myself. Not all students are that lucky. I was totally broke, so I was forced to start playing for a living. I started busking and playing with bands at night. I got gigs with pit orchestras for musical shows all over the place. I've done *Oklahoma*. I've done *Annie Get Your Gun*. I've done *Guys and Dolls*. I've done them all, purely for money. Then I started to get some of the better shows, like the pit orchestras in the Gaiety Theatre and the Olympia Theatre. And, in between, I continued to do backing vocals around Dublin with young rock bands like The Pale.' With the money she earned, Eleanor was finally in a position to purchase her beloved saxophone. 'I was also able to buy some other decent instruments for myself because I was playing on pretty rough instruments.' She told Colm O'Hare in *Hot Press* that she also performed with Phil Coulter. 'Yeah, I actually played with Phil for a long time. I was on the road with him for ages. We did a tour of the States with loads of dates – I didn't know where I was most of the time. But I've done sessions for people who wouldn't even know I played on their records, including some I wouldn't be too proud of. I've had to prostitute myself at times, but I was always glad to be able to make a living out of playing music – that was the most important thing to me.'

In 1988, Eleanor graduated from Trinity College with an honours degree in music. 'I spent a few months teaching and then auditioned for the National Symphony Orchestra. I played in RTE for three years with them. I loved that period. I loved that kind of music. I loved Mahler. I loved Mozart. It's a buzz that I miss because there's nothing like sitting in a symphony orchestra when you're in the middle of a Tchaikovsky symphony. There's nothing like that in the world. Having said that, there's nothing like standing in front of a drum kit and an electric guitar amp and a bass guitar. There's just nothing like that. It's fantastic. You can feel the bass underneath your feet. Every time they whack the snare drum or the bass drum it goes through your body. It's brilliant. But I guess my heart and soul weren't really in classical music for full-time work.'

While her main source of employment was as a violinist with the National Symphony Orchestra, Eleanor began to diversify and during that era she teamed up with the Mary Black Band, a fortuitous career move as it later transpired. After three years with the Symphony Orchestra she went on the road with Mary

Black. Watching from the wings, Eleanor took note of Mary's approach to her performance, her teamwork on stage with the band and how she communicated with the audience. The 'Mary Black university of live performing' took her around the world to America, Japan and Australia. A solid bond was established between the newcomer and the veteran singer, born out of a mutual love of music and performing. They became good friends. Mary took the fledgling under her wing and passed on her years of experience of dealing with the business side of showbusiness. She advised Eleanor on record deals and how to avoid the hidden traps that have seen many a talented artiste sign away their financial future for small returns. If Eleanor had deliberately set out to find a guru, she couldn't have crossed paths with a more suitable soul mate. When they finally reached the end of the road, Eleanor was miserable. The two women were in tears.

But Eleanor had decided that it was time to become a performer in her own right. Like any leap into the unknown, it stirred up a mixture of emotions. On the one hand there was the excitement of launching her own band. But there was also a certain amount of fear and apprehension. Was she doing the right thing? Would it all blow up in her face? But the niggling doubts soon evaporated when she immersed herself in the demanding work of rehearsing, composing and performing.

The Eleanor McEvoy Band had knitted together in a disorganised sort of fashion more like buskers teaming up than a conscious business arrangement. First came Noel Eccles on drums, who was principal percussionist in the Symphony Orchestra. He had no doubts in his mind that he wanted to perform behind Eleanor after catching an impromptu performance by her at a New Year's Eve party. Noel has worked with a range of top-notch musicians, from Van Morrison to Moving Hearts and U2. Next came Jim Tate on bass. They worked together as a three-piece unit for a year and a half. During that time Eleanor was still a member of the Symphony Orchestra and was working with Mary Black's band. 'It was hectic. Sometimes I'd be in the recording studio all night doing demo songs with my own band and then I'd go straight to the National Concert Hall to rehearse all day with the Symphony Orchestra. That night I'd go off to work with Mary. It was too much, really. It was leading to burnout. I was exhausted all the time.' Eleanor completed the line-up of her own band when Bill Shanley, a young Cork guitarist, caught her ear. Bill had been taught to play the guitar by the legendary Noel Redding, who was a member of the Jimi Hendrix Experience. 'They are all from a rock background. It's not heavy rock, but it [the band's sound] has a rock tinge to it that people initially didn't expect,' says Eleanor.

Talent scouts from a number of record companies started to pick up on the Eleanor McEvoy Band. One night when she was doing a show at the Baggot Inn rock venue in Dublin, an American holidaymaker approached her with an offer she couldn't believe. Tom Zutaut, at the time, was unknown to her. But he wasn't just any American tourist. He was a talent scout for the American record label Geffen Records and the man who had signed up Guns 'N' Roses, a heavy metal band which became world renowned. He had earlier been to Ireland and signed up the hot young rock prospects, My Little Funhouse, from Kilkenny. Zutaut, on this occasion, had taken his father to Ireland for a holiday.

'He was at a gig in Dublin one night during his visit and on the way out he got talking to the barman and some of the other people in the venue. They thought he was an American tourist and they said, "Oh, you should go down to the Baggot Inn and hear this new girl Eleanor McEvoy." He didn't know about *A Woman's Heart* at the time. He didn't know about all that side of things, which was so good for me because I wanted to make a rock album,' Eleanor later told broadcaster Brendan Balfe on RTE radio. 'At the time, I was worried that I was going to be

signed to a company that wanted twenty songs like the
"Woman's Heart". Not that I don't like the "Woman's Heart".
But it's not all I do. I do a range of rock stuff as well and I wanted
to get that through. So he came down that night and he caught
the last seven or eight songs of the gig. And he came up
afterwards to the dressing room and said, "I want to sign you."
I was a bit hesitant. I said, "Who are you?" He said, "I'm from
Geffen Records. I signed Guns 'N' Roses."'

Eleanor admits she was sceptical of Zutaut's offer at first. 'I
thought: He's American. He cannot be serious. You know the
way Americans tend to be over the top about things? But we did
take to him immediately on a personal level. He seemed to be
straightforward. He offered us more than any of the other record
companies had come up with. Geffen had a good reputation,
so we eventually signed a deal to do six albums.' It was a deal
that took the Irish rock industry by surprise, coming at a time
when many rising young rock groups had had their hopes
dashed by the crush of the recession. Groups like Cry Before
Dawn, Something Happens and A House had been dropped by
major record labels. 'I couldn't believe how lucky I was, to be
honest with you,' Eleanor confesses. 'I had friends who couldn't
meet their mortgage repayments, and I had just landed this big
contract. But, initially, all I felt was the pressure of it. I thought
the day I signed a deal it would be wonderful and I'd go out and
have a big party. I had dreamed of this all my life. But, in fact,
I felt sick. I kept thinking: Oh my God, what am I doing? But
she soon realised that the financial support from the record
company allowed her to focus on her creative work. She no
longer had to spread herself between several jobs to make ends
meet. 'It was great [the financial independence]. I never had
that before.'

Although signed to an American company, Eleanor was
determined to remain in Dublin. Geffen had asked her to make
the move to Los Angeles to record the debut album, *Eleanor*

McEvoy. But she insisted on doing it in Ireland. 'It may sound exotic to move to Los Angeles, but when you're recording you're spending fifteen hours a day in a studio. So you don't get an opportunity to see much of the outside world anyway. We eventually did the mixing in Los Angeles, but the recording was done in Dublin. There are a lot of pressures when you're recording an album, and working in familiar surroundings helps to relieve them. I could go home to my own flat and cry, or call round to my mates if things are going wrong. If I wanted a sax player I'd know who to go to in Dublin, because I know what kind of players are around. If I wanted a string section I could go to my colleagues in the orchestra. It made sense to do it in Dublin. It is possible now to live in Dublin and have your main market somewhere else. It's not as big an obstacle as it used to be.'

The personal nature of some of the songs on the album did upset her parents, Dick and Nellie McEvoy. In 'Stray Thoughts' she sings about a lover:

> *He comes to me and sets my thoughts astray*
> *He comes to chase the midnight blues away*
> *He's sweet to taste and strong to touch*
> *And I find myself inclined*
> *To hug him close and pray to God he's kind*
> *I hug him close and pray to God he's kind.*

She admits her parents find those sentiments embarrassing. 'They find it difficult. It's hard for them because they grew up in a different generation where you didn't talk about a lot of things and all of a sudden their daughter is writing songs about them. It can be difficult. But that's life. I can't compromise my songs so as not to offend. Not that I would intentionally offend anybody. I wouldn't do that. But I think the danger is always there that they are going to be a little bit offended by it. That's not my intention, but unfortunately it's sometimes the result. But if I was to avoid that I would be dishonest in my songwriting and I don't want to do that.'

Like most parents, the McEvoys had high hopes of their intelligent young daughter landing a secure, pensionable job. They wanted to see her well 'set up'. So when Eleanor dropped the bombshell that she was planning to pursue a career in music they were bitterly disappointed. 'My mother wasn't crazy about me going into music. She wanted me to go into a steady job, schoolteaching or whatever. When I went into the Symphony Orchestra, the reaction was: "Oh, that isn't very steady." But at least it was more respectable than the other end of music [rock]. But, of course, I eventually left the Symphony Orchestra and moved into rock. But now she's delighted. And so is my dad. They are delighted about the whole thing now. They really think I'm doing the right thing.'

For most mothers in Ireland, having your daughter eulogised by the country's legendary TV and radio presenter Gay Byrne lends acres of credibility to whatever career they are pursuing. And Mrs McEvoy is no exception. When Eleanor won one of the 1993 Irish entertainment awards for Best New Irish Artist, Gay Byrne was on hand to congratulate her. And sitting in the wings, watching, was an excited and proud mum, Nellie McEvoy. 'Mum came over afterwards and she had to have the pictures taken. Me and Gay Byrne. Herself and Gay Byrne. And I was going, "Oh, my God." But it was a big deal for my mum and I'm delighted to be able to do that for her.'

Both of Eleanor's parents are musical. 'They just never had a chance to do it themselves,' she says. Her sister, Marian, and brother, Kieran, both of whom are older, are also working musicians. 'My sister plays in bars around town [Dublin]. She plays piano. She's very, very musical and she writes as well. But she's more into sound engineering, that side of things. My brother, Kieran, is in a band in New York. He's playing with a girl called Dina Regine. Before that, he was with a band called Smash Gladys, a fairly well-known metal group. So he's gigging all the time as well.'

The next generation of McEvoys are also set to carry on the musical tradition. 'My sister has three children. One of them plays the fiddle and writes songs. The second one plays the clarinet and the third one plays the piano. So it is definitely in the family. My sister is the eldest. There are eleven years between me and my sister and five years between me and my brother. We are all very close. When my brother lived in Dublin he was one of my best friends. It broke my heart to see him go to the States. I really missed him. But I see him a lot now because I'm over there so much.'

Eleanor's father worked with the Department of Posts and Telegraphs, now Telecom Eireann. Retired now, he spends his time indulging his passion for oil painting. 'He's really very good at it,' says Eleanor. 'He's in exhibitions now and he's getting on really well at it. He did it years ago before he was married. Then he got married and had us and had to give it up for work commitments. It's great to see him getting back to it. It's tremendous to see him happy. For a man who wasn't happy for most of his working life, it's lovely to see him doing something that he really loves in his twilight years. I've seen a huge change in him. He's so much happier in himself. He has me looking forward to my retirement.'

Although her songs give the impression that she's a tortured soul who has had an unfair share of experiences in relationships, Eleanor reveals that she is not scarred by any of her romantic entanglements. 'I'm not really,' she laughs. 'People hear the songs and then go, "My God, she must be manic depressive." But I'm not. It's just that I write when I'm down. If there are three hours of the day that I'm feeling low, three hours of the day I'm feeling OK, three hours of the day that I'm in a party mood, I'll probably write for the three hours that I'm not feeling so hot – that I'm really low. When I'm in good form I want to go out and party. So there's an element of that. I think my experiences have been normal experiences. I don't think they've been any worse than those experienced by other people in human relationships. It's just that I'm stupid enough to write about them. I can't think of any ex-boyfriend that I don't talk to. They are my closest friends. There was one that I didn't talk to, but I made my peace with him.'

Eleanor remains tight-lipped about the identities of the former boyfriends in her songs. It's a loyalty that she will never betray. 'I have a golden rule,' she says. 'I never tell anyone who the songs are about. Nobody will ever know. Mind you, there are guys whom I've never met who claim the songs are about them! I find that really funny. But such is life.'

With world stardom beckoning as her career takes off on both sides of the Atlantic, Eleanor has been contemplating life in the public eye. 'Yeah, I think about it,' she says. 'You have to think about it because of what it brings with it. And it brings great things with it. But it brings other things that aren't so nice. In terms of being a big name, having loads of money – I want to have money. I want to be able to pay my bills. I don't want to have to worry about that. I want to be able to see a guitar that's particularly beautiful and go: Yes, I can have that. More than anything else I want to keep writing songs. Not to have to compromise myself to do certain gigs because I need the money. To be able to say: No, I don't really want to play that gig. No, I don't really want to record that acoustically. I want to do that as a rock song. If I lose some fans that's an awful pity. But this is what I want to do. To have the freedom to be able to say that.'

But fame also has a dark side. Following the success of the

Woman's Heart album and her song, 'Only A Woman's Heart', she was subjected to some hate calls. 'The fact that you're known can be great. It can be handy for some things. But it can also attract weirdos. I've had some nasty messages on my answering machine when my number was in the telephone directory. My old phone number was in the book because I'm a working musician and my work was got through the phone. When the *Woman's Heart* thing took off I got one guy who threatened to kill me. He said things like, "What would you know about a man's heart? How dare you say that kind of stuff." I also got the odd weirdo turning up at gigs. What are worse than the weirdos that don't like you are the weirdos that like you. They are even more difficult to deal with. So you have that side of things to cope with as well.'

There were also some women who suggested that 'Only A Woman's Heart' was sexist. 'In that song I'm talking about depression,' she told Joe Jackson of *The Irish Times*. 'I was asking myself, "Why am I this depressed?" I'd see a pencil fall off a table and I'd burst into tears,' Eleanor explained to Jackson. 'I'm trying to figure out if it is because some guy left me two years ago, or what? And I put the answer to that in my song by saying, "I mourn for my dreams, I mourn for my wasted love", mourn everything. That feeling still hits me and there's shag all I can do about it. But when I said, "My heart is low as only a woman's heart can be," I simply meant there is a depression that is specific to women, certainly not that it is deeper. I know men get more depressed than women. The suicide rate is higher among men than it is among women, so that's definitely not what I was saying, though, obviously, some people thought that it was. But even if I was, I'm amazed at people going on about how "Only A Woman's Heart" is sexist. I'd spent my life listening to songs that are sexist, like "T'Aint Nobody's Business If I Do", where the singer says, "I would rather my man to hit me, Than for him to jump up and quit me." That's certainly been the dominant mode of expression in the blues and in rock 'n' roll.' When Mary Coughlan recorded 'T'Ain't Nobody's Business', she refused to sing the lines quoted here. Would Eleanor refuse? 'The original song has a woman saying, "I love this guy so much, I'll stay with him even if he hits me, that's how desperate I am." That's an honest emotion and if you change that lyric you change the statement in the entire song so, no, I couldn't do that. And the point is, there are women who feel that way. I wouldn't. I'd walk.'

Despite the hate calls from some males who were fired up with rage by the lyrics in 'Only A Woman's Heart', Eleanor stresses that she personally doesn't hate men. 'I don't hate men. I love men. That's my problem,' she laughs. But she does feel that there is a feminist aspect to the success of the *Woman's Heart* album, that the anti-male brigade were out in force to snap it up. 'Sometimes "Only A Woman's Heart" gets branded into that category, which is not really what I'm about. I hate the fact that sometimes the anti-man thing comes across. At the same time, I think it's great to see six women achieving that kind of success. We are all doing our different thing and it's great that it is all women and we need to celebrate that. It would be great to see more women making their mark in bands. Where are all the female drummers? Women should be playing guitars. I do think a certain amount of it is conditioning. I know it's not easy to get out there when there's nobody else up there doing it. You have to cope with the comments in an all-male band when you're on the road [touring]. It's difficult going on the road with twenty-three men for six weeks. When you have to stop the van at four o'clock in the morning to go to the loo ...'

As a female musician in a predominantly male world, Eleanor told *Hot Press* that she experienced the usual prejudices. 'In the Mary Black Band I was a fiddle and keyboard player as well as doing backing vocals. At one particular venue down the country, the sound guy was setting up the levels before the gig and I was at my keyboards pressing a few buttons and playing a bit, the usual thing before a show. Suddenly he started shouting at me, "Don't touch that!" I looked at him, wondering what the hell was going on. "You're over there," he said, pointing. "No, I'm here," I said, "that's my microphone." "Oh, all right," he sighed, and proceeded to pick up my microphone from behind the keyboard and move it over to the other side of the stage. So I said to him, "How am I going to play and sing at the same time?" It was only then it dawned on me that he didn't realise I was the keyboard player – he thought I was just a backing singer. It never entered his head that I might be a musician as well as a singer. That kind of thing can be really annoying, though it doesn't happen that often, thankfully.'

As she steers a course through the often murky waters of showbusiness, Eleanor McEvoy has one main strength in her favour. It's her all-consuming passion for music. She has yet to find a substitute for the buzz it generates within her. Music is her drug, her love, her driving force. 'Music is my life,' she admits. 'I have nothing else in my life. I only have music. I don't have a television. I don't go out. I don't have a social life outside of music. I do go to hear other bands. I'd love to go to films, but I don't have the time. Music is my life and, given that it's my life, I have to have a lot of variety in music. I found that when I was playing in the Symphony Orchestra I'd come home and start playing rock music. I'd put on the Rolling Stones *Steel Wheels*. Now I come home and I put on classical music all the time. It's really weird. But I think you need extremes of music if you have nothing else in your life. Certainly, I do. People often ask, "Do you not get sick of music?" I used to pretend to people, "Ah yes, sometimes I do." But I don't. I never get sick of it.'

Eleanor writes in one of her songs, 'Breathing Hope', that music can be the panacea for our troubles and our ills:

I heard the music lighting up my darkness
I felt the phrase melt away my sadness
A melody as potent as wine
I let it sweep me out of my depression
I let it point me in a new direction
Breathing hope on this life of mine.

She wrote 'Breathing Hope' when, she says, 'the beauty of music struck me one day, as it does many days. It's about the healing power of music. That it can breathe hope into your life. It can heal you. You hear a melody as potent as wine and you're on a high from the melody. You're on a high from a lyric. You go, "Yes, that's exactly how I felt," and it's the same high you get from having a glass or two of wine. And sometimes it's a better buzz. The melody as potent as wine.'

DOLORES KEANE

DOLORES KEANE

Fame crept up on Dolores Keane like frost in the night. In her formative years as a child, Dolores's background was a natural breeding ground for a career in music. A career that would eventually take her away from her simple but happy rural environment to a jet-set lifestyle performing around the world. Looking back on her early life as a youngster growing up in Caherlistrane, County Galway, Dolores, who was reared in her grandparents' home, recalls how there were seemingly endless days and nights of music and *craic* in the house. For Dolores, steeped in that musical tradition and atmosphere, singing was a way of life and it became a talent that she took for granted. When the likeable performer became a fully fledged 'personality' years later after gradually establishing herself as a first-class singing talent on the home scene, she reacted to her star status with bemusement.

'I've never looked upon myself as a star,' Dolores said in a special interview for this book. 'It's not a term I would apply to myself. I don't see myself as being different to anyone else. But sometimes it does strike me that what I do causes a ripple. It might hit me at the launch of one of my albums when I look around and say to myself, "There's Mary Black and there's Ronan Collins and Derek Davis and Thelma Mansfield and they're all here because I'm here." Sometimes it strikes me like that. Journalists often ask me how I started my career and when I realised it was a success. But to me it was a very natural thing to sing. I never decided to be a singer. It came to me like talking and walking and eating your dinner. But, of course, as your popularity grows it does become a career. You realise that when you're out on tour for weeks, away from home and working hard. That's when it dawns on you that this is work.'

Today, Dolores Keane's life as a singer is light years away from her background rooted in the traditions and customs of a bygone era. Way back then she enjoyed a simple country existence. 'It was a good part of the world to grow up in if you had an interest in music,' she recalls. 'There were lots of singers and musicians and storytellers around that area during my childhood. It was not uncommon for one of them to drop in with a new song and start off a *seisiún* in the house. That was a regular event way back then.'

Her father, 'Big Matt' Keane, was a member of The Keanes' Céilí Band, which also featured her aunts, Rita and Sarah, and uncles, Tom, John Joe and Paddy and Tom Hynes, a friend and musician from Tuam. Big Matt, as he was known to family and friends because of his height and impressive physique, initially supported his family as an employee of the local 'big house'. He worked for General Bernard of Castlehackett Estate where he was in charge of the buying and selling of stock. Dolores remembers 'The General' as 'a big man who wore tweed suits and was a real country squire. He was very good to all his employees. He treated them with a lot of dignity and respect and they loved him for it. When The General died they all went to the funeral and my father was one of the men who carried the coffin. But at Mass the following Sunday they were all denounced from the altar by the local priest. He told them they would no longer be welcome in his church for going to a Protestant funeral. That was the attitude they had back in those days. You dared not go into a Protestant church in those times.' The General left Dolores's father and mother his big brass bed in his will. Big Matt went on to work on a building site in Galway and later became a truck driver. The céilí band was a sideline activity and one he revelled in. In the fifties and sixties the Keane family travelled all around Galway playing at weddings and 'American wakes' – going-away parties for locals who were emigrating to the States.

When she was four years old, Dolores left the family home in Castlehackett and went to live with her grandparents, Mattie, also known as Big Matt, and May Keane and her aunts and uncles four miles away in Caherlistrane. She explains that it was quite normal in those times for children to leave their parents, brothers and sisters and move in with their grandparents, aunts and uncles. 'It's a tradition, I'm sure, that was not peculiar to the west of Ireland. Children from large families often went to live with their grandparents,' Dolores says. 'I liked living on the farm with my aunts, uncles and my grandparents and because I was mad into music and there were so many *seisiúns* in the house I enjoyed being there. I started off spending a lot of time with them and eventually I stayed with them full-time. Anyway, I wasn't a hundred miles away from my immediate family because my parents, brothers and sisters only lived a few miles up the road.'

Her grandparents' home in Caherlistrane is a thatched house with an open hearth fire where traditional Irish cooking is still carried on. Looking back on her childhood growing up on the one-hundred-acre farm, Dolores describes it as 'a lovely time in my life'. Apart from her passion for music, Dolores also has a penchant for food and she has fond memories of delicious meals in the middle of the day in Caherlistrane. Today, cooking is one of her favourite pastimes. 'I was brought up on cabbage, bacon and spuds. The main meal would be served in the middle of the day because work on the farm started in the early morning. It was usually cabbage, bacon and spuds and to this day I still love green cabbage and fat bacon. I also love crubeens [pigs' feet] and lambs' tails. Lambs' tails are a delicacy. But they're a lot of bother. You have to clip off the wool and then you have to burn the tail in the fire. Another favourite meal was a fish called ling, which was eaten with fried potatoes. It was salted and preserved because people in the west of Ireland didn't have fridges in those days. They used to salt a lot of the fish, except for Fridays when a van would come round with fresh herrings and mackerel to the door. My grandmother had fabulous recipes and ways of cooking. She would never gut a herring before cooking it, for instance. Herring is a very dry fish, so she'd cook it whole and then gut it. It would be served with white sauce, potatoes and parsley. You wouldn't get a meal like it today. I absolutely adore the TV chef Keith Floyd. But he has still never come up with the recipes that I have, so I feel I have one up on him! At Christmas, of course, the goose would be cooked in the hearth and the bread was always baked in a pot oven over the open fire. It's still baked the same way today by Rita and Sarah. Most of the cooking is done over the open fire. They can do anything there.

The *seisiúns* in my grandparents' home would vary. The locals came in a lot of nights during the week and there was a lot of storytelling. Someone might drop in on their way home from town and ask, "Did you ever hear this song?" That kind of thing would start up an evening of music and song that would continue into the early hours of the morning.'

Rita and Sarah Keane, Dolores's two aunts, had become well known among traditional music lovers around Europe, America and Canada – long before Dolores herself emerged as a major talent. They released an album which was well received and broadened their appeal. This resulted in an influx of traditional fans into Ireland to hear more of the Keane sisters. The *seisiúns* in the Keane home soon became a cosmopolitan gathering.

'During the summers a lot of people would come from England, France, Germany and Canada, people who had heard about Rita and Sarah when their album came out and others we met at *Fleadh Cheoils*. They'd come to the house and stay for a weekend or a week,' Dolores remembers. 'It sparked off mini-*fleadheanna*, with *seisiúns* going on during the day, the night and often into the next morning. Everyone who came helped out on the farm during the day and that meant that the work was finished earlier in the evening and the *craic* could start sooner. You would find flute players and other gifted musicians with welts and blisters on their hands from forking hay and oats and the like. Of course, they loved it because they lived in cities, so it was a novelty. The house isn't a big house and there was no way we could accommodate all the musicians, so they would come equipped with tents. There would be a little village of tents up the field during the summer months. You'd never know what kind of a musician would come out of a tent at night, but they'd all come into the house for the *seisiún* and they were all welcome. There would be plenty of brown bread, which Sarah would have baked over the fire. And of course there was local *poitín*. That kind of scene went on for three months over the summer period.'

One of Dolores's earliest memories is of the late Willie Clancy, a man regarded as one of the master pipers of this century, performing in the house. 'He sat inside the house one night and I'll never forget the way he played. The music he made was out of this world. Most of the modern performers of today, people on the international scene, wouldn't be in the same league as Willie Clancy because their love isn't in the music. Music has to come from the heart and the soul. I feel that nowadays videos and technology in general are destroying the music. And if what you're singing or what you're playing doesn't come from your heart, as far as I'm concerned it's not good music. Willie Clancy still stands out in my mind for the magic he weaved that night. And I found him to be a most placid man and the most beautiful man you could meet.'

Being at the core of that type of musical activity as a youngster and exposed to a diverse range of talented artistes, Dolores was treated to an education that she could never have found in any formal musical institution. The beauty of it all is that she wasn't even aware of the fact that her talent as a singer was being gradually honed and cultivated. Her singing was developing in the most natural way possible. And she soaked up every delicious moment of it. She became accustomed to performing in public and outside of home when she took part in *Fleadhanna Ceoil* and entered competitions. Not surprisingly her talent didn't go unnoticed and she notched up three All Ireland titles for traditional singing.

While her early life on the farm was for the most part a fairytale existence, Dolores has memories of times when the work was gruelling. 'When I was going to school the sugar beet factory was in Tuam and all around that area was booming at the time. But one of the chores I had on the farm was to pull beet by hand. It was harvested in November and December when the weather was bitterly cold and the frost would be crippling your hands. The plough would go along under the beet and you'd attempt to pull it, but sometimes it wouldn't come with you. Then suddenly it would and you'd end up on your back in the muck. You'd be cold, wet and miserable. It was awful cold, awful, awful cold. Some of the harvesting was done by night because whenever the beet factory decided that they wanted the beet you had to work towards that deadline. But I never complained because my elders were doing it, so why should I complain? Spreading the slits, which was planting potatoes, was another back-breaking chore. It was also done by hand from a pouch around your waist. To ease the burden going along a drill we'd hum a song to get a rhythm going in the work. Although it was tough work, I often wish I was back in those days. I've often hankered after those simple times and the physical work and somebody else having to worry about where the next few quid was going to come from. The people in Ireland have gone the other way now. They don't even grow their own vegetables. Even if they only had a square inch outside they could grow herbs. I love gardening. It's one of the great pleasures I enjoy when I'm at home. Unfortunately, it's not easy for me to run a garden nowadays because I'm away on tour quite a lot and it gets out of hand.'

Dolores attended the Presentation Convent in Tuam for her secondary education. She says she now regrets the fact that she didn't sit her Leaving Certificate examination. 'I wanted to do art, maths and Irish as honours subjects. I was mad into art. I won the first prize in Connaught in an art competition run in conjunction with Conservation Year. But the school didn't have a teacher to teach me honours art, so I had to take that class in the Mercy Convent, along with three other students from my own school. Travelling between the two schools, we were regularly late for classes in both places and I became very disillusioned with the whole thing. The Christmas before the Leaving Cert I decided that I wasn't going back to school, so I opted out.'

She did a secretarial course and secured a job as a typist with an American factory in Tuam, but her love of music remained a force in her life and at the age of seventeen, while holding down her day job, Dolores joined De Danann. At the time the group consisted of Johnny McDonagh, Frankie Gavin, Alec Finn and Charlie Pickett. 'Johnny asked me if I would join the group, but because I was only seventeen at the time my family didn't agree to it. They weren't happy about me touring around the country with a group of men. But when they got to know the band they realised that they were lovely people. They are very good friends of mine to this day. I've never had a falling out with them.' Working with De Danann was, she says, 'the first time I ever sang accompanied and it was at that stage I realised how much I enjoyed singing and how I would like to do it full-time. The American company closed and went off, as American companies do. Then I started to work in the Tuam-based potato plant, Erin Foods, both in the office and on the factory floor. All the time I was playing with De Danann, but just doing two gigs a week.'

Fate intervened and her life took a new turn with the arrival in Caherlistrane of BBC TV presenter John Faulkner. 'I met John when he came over to Ireland to make a film for the BBC on traditional music. John and his colleague Nigel Williams came to Caherlistrane to record Rita and Sarah. I remember being very impressed by him. John is English and he's a musician and songwriter. He was a member of Ewan MacColl's group at one stage.' Romance blossomed between Dolores and John and soon she found herself working as a freelance researcher on music-related shows for the BBC with a number of different producers, including John.

One assignment took her to Canada where she worked on two documentaries relating to emigration. 'They dealt with the people who were there, the songs that were there and how much of the tradition was still alive.' She recalls tracking down songs and singers during her stint in Newfoundland. It was so cold that even the sea was frozen over. Dolores remembers her detective work leading her to one local singer, but he refused to meet her. She assumed he thought she was working for the inland revenue, but after driving through the snow she was determined to get her man and her song. 'I stormed up to his back door and knocked on it and I shouted, "I'm from Ireland. There's no problem. I'm a singer myself." Obviously hearing the accent helped him to change his mind about me and he eventually came out and sang the version of the song I was chasing.'

Back in England, Dolores married John Faulkner in 1977. The couple regularly performed together on the London scene, but eventually decided to move to Ireland. Dolores had been over seven years out of the country when she returned at the end of 1980. 'We bought a thatched cottage and we did it up. John is very good at woodwork.' They lived close to Rita and Sarah, and Dolores remembers many happy times going out fishing in the evenings and, as darkness descended, heading down to Canavan's of Belclare for a few pints. That's the sort of lifestyle she enjoys, she says.

Upon her return to Ireland, Dolores found herself back in the ranks of De Danann, where she teamed up with Mary Black, their lead singer at the time. 'I had a great time with them,' she says. 'Who wouldn't? Mary Black is such a fabulous person. Mary and her sister, Frances, are among my favourite people.' But eventually she left De Danann and headed up a group which included her husband, John. 'I felt at that stage that there were a lot of different songs that I wanted to do. And I wanted to work with a different band. It was something I personally needed to get out of my system. I had a yearning to be known as a contemporary singer, as opposed to a traditional singer or a folk singer, even though I had been quite successful in that scene. Of course, I still sing traditional songs on stage and still sing songs that I had learned from Rita and Sarah. They were a major influence on me when I was growing up. I always remember singing with Rita and Sarah. To this day, I simply adore those two people.'

In an *RTE Guide* interview, Dolores told Paddy Kehoe that her family are her biggest critics. 'They'd be awful proud, like, of what I'd be doing and that, but if I was singing something they didn't like, I'd be told that as well – oh, no quicker! "What kind of a song is that, where did you get that? No, I didn't like that now!" Rita and Sarah said they didn't like a version of "The Raggle Taggle Gypsy-O" called "The Dark-Eyed Gypsy-O". I remember them mentioning that they weren't too wild into that, they thought that it didn't really suit me.' Does she still do the song? 'Not at all,' she laughs. 'You must be joking. I have to live there.'

While admitting that it is more difficult for women to forge ahead with a high-powered career, particularly if they decide to combine it with motherhood and the demands that that entails, Dolores disagrees with the argument that men are totally responsible for preventing women achieving their full potential. She doesn't blame men for the fact that only a small number of women of her generation have blazed a trail to reach dizzy heights on the Irish music scene. 'I don't honestly think that the lack of women going out on the road or anything else has anything to do with men. It was just something that women didn't do years back, although my aunts played in a *céilí* band for years. But women in general just didn't have the courage or conviction way back then to take that step. I don't think it was a case that the men were making if difficult for them. Of course, it's the women who have the babies and usually they're the ones that look after the kids while the men go out to work. But if the women were really determined about a career they could have found ways of organising their lives to combine the two. I did it. I had a nanny looking after our son, Joseph, for a few years because John and I went away working together. My sister also looked after him whenever we had to go away on trips. It's difficult. There's no two ways about it, it is difficult because you're torn between the two. You think, I have a certain talent. I can go out and I can sing and it's something I very much enjoy. If you're in the arts, whether it's music or whatever, and you have that longing inside you to do it, then you're pushed by that all the time anyway. I wouldn't speak for Mary Black, but I'm sure she's the same way. It's not that we had to work, but you enjoy making your own mark.

'When women like Mary Black and Maura O'Connell and myself started making our way in the music business, no man ever pointed the finger and said: You're a woman. You're entering a man's world. I don't think it was ever a man's world. I don't think it was ever a question of that. My grandmother was brought up in a farming community and she was the one in the house who held the purse strings. My grandfather was the one who went out and did the manual work on the land. But whenever anything was sold, she looked after the money. When he went to town on a Saturday to get the supplies in the horse and cart, she was the one who said, "We can afford for you to have a few pints." If you want to do something, do it. There's no point saying in twenty years time, "I would have done that if it wasn't for ..." I think that's a really stupid attitude to have. You can't live your life on someone else's back. If you do you're going to end up a very, very unhappy person. That doesn't apply only to women. There are a lot of men out there who never made a go of anything because they didn't have what it takes to get out and do it.'

Dolores doesn't see the *Woman's Heart* album as women flying the flag, taking a stand and making their mark. It was simply a concept album of six high-profile Irish female artistes. A very good idea that caught the imagination of the public and rocketed up the charts, achieving the type of success that no one had ever envisaged. 'We are six female performers who have our own individual following. But to find that kind of success in a small island like Ireland is incredible. I'm amazed by it. It was great doing the tour and great working with the girls again. I had worked with Mary in De Danann about ten years previously. We immediately hit it off and really got to know each other during that period. We worked on a De Danann album *Anthem* together. Mary and myself did "Diglake Fields" and I did "Anthem for Ireland" and "Let It Be".

'We both had the *craic* working together and became great friends. When we went out to tour the *Woman's Heart* album, it was great to find that the audiences were there *all* the time. It was great for live music because it got people out to gigs again in Ireland. A lot of venues on that first tour wouldn't have had big crowds for years because of the recession. But the fans came out in their thousands. We couldn't believe it. We were amazed by it.'

Despite the fact that the four women who toured the album, Dolores, Maura O'Connell, Frances Black and Eleanor McEvoy all have their own individual status to maintain, there was no haggling over who topped the bill on the night. 'There's very little begrudgery between bands or singers in this country and I think that's lovely,' Dolores says. 'There was no question of Maura O'Connell being top of the bill or of myself being top of the bill. We juggled it around. There was no problem. There was a great rapport between the four of us and we really enjoyed it.'

In her personal life, Dolores has suffered the heartache of a failed marriage. 'I think we just drifted apart,' she reflects, trying desperately to analyse how it went wrong. 'Maybe, in a sense, the business we were both in and being together all the time didn't help either. But, then again, I don't know, because we never had any major rows about the musical aspect. It's something I'll probably work out in years to come. But I can't give a straight answer right now. It's quite a recent thing and I'm still scarred, as I'm sure John is. I find it difficult now talking about it, because it's only when I talk about it that I realise it actually happened and it's there. But at least we have managed to remain friends and we are still playing together in the band. There are no problems in that regard. It's the way we both wanted it. There's no animosity. No malice. Nothing like that there. I don't believe you can live with a person for fifteen years, which is the period John and I were together, and just write that off or get someone to write it off. We didn't get into that kind of thing [legally], which I'm delighted about and I know John is too. It's great that we are both continuing on together professionally because John has always been part of the music and he's been in various groups with me down through the years.' While she respects the institution of marriage, Dolores does feel that divorce should be available to people in this country who find themselves in her situation.

Having come to terms with the fact that she's now a major singing star, instantly recognised wherever she goes in Ireland, Dolores has learned to enjoy it. 'I still find it strange the way people react to me because to me it's a natural thing to sing. But I'm always delighted when people come up to me to say how much they enjoy the songs that I sing and, obviously, I'm very pleased when I get good crowds at concerts. When there's a gig or a concert tour I go out and do them. And when I go home you'll find me out digging the garden, or hanging out with Rita and Sarah, doing the shopping, normal things like that.' She remains very close to her family. Dolores has two sisters, Christina and Teresa, who are both married with children and who also like to sing at *seisiúns*. She has four brothers: Big Matt 'who takes on the responsibility of the clan and who would organise a session in the Sahara;' Noel, who plays the flute and accordion; Pat 'who is a different singer to the rest of us – you should hear him sing "Mona Lisa". He has an incredible voice. It's like no one that I've heard;' and Seán, who is the only professional performer among the brothers. Her mother Bridie is still alive, but her father, Matt, has passed on. 'My father was one of the best people that I've ever known,' Dolores says. 'When I think back on my early years, there was always equality in our house. Sunday was always my mother's day off. My father used to always get the Sunday dinner. Big Matt was very romantic. He used to bring her flowers, or if he was in Dublin and saw a dress that he thought would look good on Bridie, he'd buy it. Nothing was too good for Bridie as far as he was concerned. It was a real love story. You wouldn't see it in the movies. He had a tremendous influence on me. Big Matt had a great love for nature and was big into conservation. He had a great regard for wildlife, as I do.'

Even though she was reared by her grandmother and aunts,

Dolores maintained a very strong bond with her mother. Bridie, she says, was an extremely liberal woman. Whenever she needed advice or support, Dolores would always turn to her mother or her aunts, Rita and Sarah. She does have a spiritual side to her life: 'I do pray. I do go to Mass, but I don't go around wearing all these things on my sleeve. I don't talk about them a lot because I like to keep my personal life as personal as I can. God knows, I don't have an awful lot of my personal life that is personal.'

On the music front, Dolores feels that her art is currently enjoying a very healthy climate. 'People are more aware now, for sure, of the different music that's out there,' she told *Hot Press*. 'I think it was never as healthy as it is now. Especially for traditional music because ten or fifteen years ago people would have thought of it as being really old fashioned. It's really the in-thing now. It's cool, man!' She says that travelling has broadened her outlook on life. 'I love meeting people so that wide experience has to have an influence.' Her confidence has grown over the years to such an extent that she is no longer shy about singing songs that would have been decried by the purists of Irish traditional music and perhaps also by the 'lace curtain' Irish who associated it with the peasantry, although she told Seán Boyne of *The Sunday World* that in her family, steeped in the *sean nós* tradition as it is, there was never any conflict between the pure culture and the popular ballads of the people. 'I know now and I've proven to myself that I can sing different types of songs, but as well as that I know that I can sing them with conviction. If I wanted to sing a song like Stevie Winwood's "The Finer Things" one time, I would have only done it in a session. I wouldn't ever have dreamt of doing it on stage or recording it because I was basically known as a traditional singer and I would have been worried about what the tradition-alists would feel about me singing a song like that. But I just had to say to myself one day: Look, I have to do this for me. If I'm not happy with what I'm doing then I'm not going to produce anything that's worthwhile for anyone else to appreciate.'

Today, Dolores says she's happy in her life, both professionally and on a personal level. But she does admit to being saddened and disillusioned with the way human beings are treating their environment and the manner in which they are destroying nature and making many species of birds and animals extinct. Having grown up on a farm, Dolores remains very close to nature and she still hankers after the days when life seemed to be simpler. When she contemplates the 'rat race' and the pressures that modern life rains down on people today, Dolores's thoughts wander back to the long hot summers on the farm in Caherlistrane, the music in the house and the bread baking over the fire. As a woman who is not afraid to show her emotions, the memories bring tears to her eyes. Living in the past is where Dolores Keane is happiest.

MAURA O'CONNELL

MAURA O'CONNELL

Nashville was never on Maura O'Connell's mind when she was growing up in Ennis, County Clare. Country music certainly didn't have a place in her life. On the contrary, she despised it. The irony of this is that now she has made her home in, and works out of the country music capital of the world – Nashville, Tennessee. 'If anyone had said to me ten years ago that I would even go to Nashville, never mind end up working there, I would have laughed at them,' she says today.

Growing up in Ennis, an area steeped in traditional Irish music, Maura knew from an early age that she was a singer. In that close-knit community she was afforded every opportunity to display her singing ability at local concerts and functions. Locals who could sing were encouraged to do so. 'In the locality where I grew up you'd have an intrinsic knowledge of what your talent was. Whether you were prepared to face it or not was another thing. I knew I could sing. One never gets up on stage unless one knows that one can [sing]. The going on stage bit was just a fear I had to get over. That's the wonderful thing about Ireland. That's the gift Ireland has. It nurtures talent in an amateur way. Or, at least it used to.' The daughter of a local fishmonger, Frank O'Connell, Maura is not the only member of the family to have a lovely voice. Her late mother, Amby, had long established her reputation around Ennis as having a voice to kill for. 'She was an incredible talent. A beautiful soprano,' Maura recalls. 'She sang in the operas and in the choirs and in the parochial concerts and she never got paid a pound for it. I have three sisters and they are wonderful singers, although they never pursued it as a career. It was a way of life in our household. We all sang. We had our little party pieces. Any time there was a gathering we sang. Even when we were washing the dishes we'd have the radio on or the record player on and we'd be dancing and singing, that is, when we weren't fighting, because I went through a normal family life.' Music has been her main source of support throughout her life. She once had a summer run in Bunratty Castle as one of the Bunratty singers. 'I was about eighteen or nineteen and it was fun,' she says. 'At the time, I was a kind of a hippy. At least I thought I was. I wanted to be a hippy and I dressed like one. So it was very different.'

Her foray into the music scene as a professional artiste began in earnest when she teamed up with another young Ennis musician, Mike Hanrahan, who later went on to make his mark in the business with Stockton's Wing. At the time, folk music was in vogue and there was a plethora of folk clubs enjoying tremendous support. 'It was a very lively scene,' Maura remembers. One night, Maura went along to one of the folk clubs to sing. 'They had an amateur night and I remember exactly what I sang: "Soldier On"; the Thom Moore song ["Midnight Well"]; "It's Going To Be Easy from Now On", a Carlene Carter song; and "Boulder to Bermingham", the Emmylou Harris song about Gram Parsons. T.V. Honan [a local impresario] saw me perform and he teamed me up with Mike Hanrahan.

'So the two of us made a tape for our own curiosity and we called it The Sea of My Imagination. It was for ourselves and we gave copies to our parents. Then we started doing gigs together. On our very first gig we opened for Barry Moore [Christy Moore's brother, now known as Luka Bloom]. It was at a benefit gig for Carnsore Point.' Ollie Jennings, a well known Galway promoter, former manager of De Danann and the man behind the success of The Sawdoctors, regularly invited Maura and Mike to perform at Smokey Joe's, a club in University College

Galway. The duo would usually go on to warm up the crowd before the headline act. 'That was a very magical time for me musically,' Maura recalls. 'We were singing for the pure, sheer love of it. It wasn't our career.' Although she was unaware of it at the time, Maura was serving her apprenticeship in the trade. 'One of the highlights of my career was singing with Mike Hanrahan and getting my first review.'

Ollie Jennings played a major role in the development of Maura's career. In 1980 the manager of De Danann teamed her up with his group after they heard her singing at a party one night and were struck by the quality of her voice. It was a partnership that led to a two-year touring stint with one of the most influential and successful groups of the day. Maura could hardly believe her good fortune. Her career rocketed and she found herself jet-setting around the world. 'It was so exciting being in New York and Los Angeles. I was like a kid jumping up and down. I was zapped by the whole thing.' That first tour of the States back in the early eighties was on the back of her first hit single, 'My Irish Molly-O!'. Although she wasn't aware of it then, Maura's introduction to America would eventually alter the course of her life, musically as well as personally.

After two years with De Danann, Maura decided to leave to pursue a solo career. She soon discovered, however, that there are both advantages and disadvantages to being an artiste in Ireland. On the one hand, because it's such a small territory, it's not that difficult to become a big fish in a small pond. But because it has a very small touring circuit, there is always the danger that an artiste can be over-exposed to the public and the familiarity factor can be the death knell for any performer. Like many well known singers and groups, Maura learned that you can be a household name in Ireland and not have a penny to your name at the same time. 'There were many, many times I wished I had a job that would actually pay money,' she says. And, in an interview with Richie Taylor of *The Sunday Press*, she admitted that one of the reasons she finally made the full-time move to Nashville was because she felt she had gone as far as she could go in this country. 'When I lived here I was as famous as I could be, but I was also as broke as I could be,' she told Taylor. She also believed that she fell off the 'popularity wave' in Ireland for a few years in the mid-eighties. 'I was completely unhip there for quite some time. The whole idea of a singer without some sort of image was gone. The rock scene took over and it wouldn't have done me any good to stay. I would have ended up playing late-night dances, which would probably have seen me attacking the audience with a machete.'

It was music producer and broadcaster P.J. Curtis who introduced her to Nashville. 'I went to the university of whatever is music to P.J. for a couple of years in Clare. He taught me so much. He had an incredible collection of records. I used to go up to him once a week and he'd play me everything, right across the broad musical spectrum, from soul to country. It was the really good stuff. The top end. And he would quiz me about them the following week. He'd nearly ask me who was eating the sandwich in the control room when the song was being recorded. P.J. knew many people in Nashville and he said to me, "Come on out to Nashville." But at the time I thought, Oh, my goodness, Nashville means X, Y and Z and if you add them all up I'll be a country singer and I'm not wearing cowboy suits for anyone. I had had an abhorrence of country music and everything that was to do with Nashville. But it was P.J. who broke down that prejudice, plus the fact that I had heard people like Emmylou Harris and Gram Parsons – more that side of the country music thing. But to me, Nashville was somewhere they all had absconded from and gone to Los Angeles and Texas.

'I eventually went off to Nashville because P.J. assured me that things were a little bit different there.' She told Brendan Balfe on RTE radio: 'I really only went over to demo some songs, check it out, see what was going on and we ended up recording the bones of my first album. When I came back home to do the album, country music was still very unhip in Ireland and just the very name Nashville was a turn-off. So I went on a bender. I died my hair all the colours of the rainbow and put a soul band together, just in case anybody, even myself, would know what I was doing. I found that if you don't write the material, whatever you did last is what people think you are. There were so many other aspects to my musical personality, I was trying not to get labelled. So I went on a bender. But then I relaxed. Then I went back to Nashville to record my next album, *Just In Time*, because I really wanted to get back to basics. Back to a very simple sound. So we did old songs like, "If You Love Me" and we had a hit with "Feet Of A Dancer". I found that there was fertile ground for musicians and singers like myself in Nashville.'

A chance meeting with a group called the New Grass Revival at a festival in Kentucky while she was performing with De Danann later played a role in cementing her relationship with Nashville. 'Because I'd known the guys [New Grass Revival] living there, I knew there was some value to it [Nashville],' she says. 'I did like country music at the time, but it was country music coming out of L.A. It was the more forward stuff like Emmylou Harris and Gram Parsons that took my interest, more than the standard type of country music that I didn't care for very much.' She told Helena Mulkearns of *The Irish Times*: 'A lot of the reasons why I came here [Nashville] had to do with the musicians I met, like Jerry Douglas, Edgar Meyer, Russ Barenberg, all of whom are musicians who are not bound by what people think, who just genuinely love music.'

In an interview for this book, she adds: 'When I went there, I found that there was a very interesting music scene going on that wasn't centred around the country music, in that the instrumentation that I was interested in at the time were the more acoustic traditional instruments like the banjo and the Dobro and the fiddle and the string bass. They had transcended the instruments to become musicians in their own right and that almost symbolically made me feel very comfortable there, because I wanted to transcend the constraints of being a particular kind of singer. And, for me it was very good to go over there and see that kind of openness among a community that is considered to be closed. I felt very much at home.'

Romance also played a role in nurturing her love for Nashville. She struck up a relationship with a Nashville musician, banjoist Bela Fleck. This led to regular visits to the country capital. 'So it was more for fun that I was going back for a lot of the time,' she admits. Eventually the relationship fizzled out, but they are still friends. 'Then I started making my records there and started working with Jerry Douglas, Edgar Meyer and Russ Barenberg. They are all very well known in the acoustic music scene. And it was really through them and through their entrée there and through their kudos that I started to get known, and Warner Brothers record company thought: Well, if they like her she must be pretty good, so they started looking at me. It was a question of being in the right place at the right time.'

It was a courageous move to leave Ireland where she enjoyed celebrity status, to build her career from the ground again as an unknown. 'In a way it was refreshing,' she says. 'I wanted to do different things and I didn't want there to be too many preconceptions when I started. I found it very exciting and I've been very lucky. But I worked in Ireland for a long time to support my being able to go out and start from the bottom in America. So I have a lot to thank Ireland for. I was given a very privileged entry into Nashville though, because I was going in as friends of those guys [Douglas, Meyer, Barenberg]. I can't say that if someone went over in the morning without contacts that it would work out. I was very lucky because I was in the situation where I wasn't looking for a country deal. I wasn't really in competition with anybody. I was able to stand above the crowd because of my associations and because I was Irish as well.

There are not too many Irish singers in Nashville.'

Maura has achieved critical acclaim since moving to Nashville. Her second album, *Helpless Heart,* was nominated for a Grammy Award in 1990. That's something she's particularly pleased about as a non-writer because she believes that singers who don't compose their own work have long been regarded as some kind of inferior being. 'I've encountered that kind of attitude since I started singing,' she told Joe Jackson of *Hot Press,* 'as have people like Mary Black. I've talked to her about it and although we understand how it happened, we both hate that prejudice. Prior to the sixties, the songwriter was the low man on the totem pole, the song was always associated with the singer and never with its writer. Bob Dylan changed all this, giving rightful credit to the songwriter. But the negative effect is that those of us who followed him, and didn't write their own material, were regarded as inferior and not worthy of really listening to. This is particularly true of women, very few of whom have written their own songs. So it has taken thirty years for the singer to redefine his or her position in popular music. That's why, although I love Bob Dylan songs like "You Gonna Make Me Lonesome When You Go", I hate what he did to music on that level.' She admits that it took her quite a few years to find her own confidence musically and the Grammy Award was the boost she needed. 'It did make me think that I wasn't being naive to think I could make valid, personal, artistic statements through albums of songs a singer carefully chooses, rather than songs she writes. I've always viewed my work that way, whether I was covering pop, country, Irish, whatever. I always felt that if the song reflects something true in my life it might have a similar kind of meaning for listeners.'

In recent years, Nashville has begun to stamp its mark on the world music scene again. The music coming out of the country capital has crossed over to new audiences and is no longer regarded as unfashionable. Maura O'Connell is now in the right place at the right time. She's one of the new breed of Nashville performers who are setting the scene alight. People like Garth Brooks, Randy Travis, Vince Gill, Mary Chapin Carpenter have injected new life back into the Nashville scene. 'It's a completely different city to when I moved there initially, or to when I first went there,' she says. 'I first went over there in 1983, but I didn't actually move there until 1986. And the difference is the boomtown that it has become in terms of music. It has always been a very interesting place. And it has always been more progressive than anyone has ever imagined. The explosion that has come out of there is because there has been a great fermenting. People like Mary Chapin Carpenter and Vince Gill are exceptionally talented artistes. Now it's great to be there because there are these wonderful people and they are doing great. That isn't to say that there aren't things that don't slip through every now and again. But there are some wonderful things that have happened and it has changed so much it's hard to imagine what it was like.'

Although based in Nashville, Maura spends her time on the road performing all over the States, occasionally returning to Ireland for shows. 'I'm a touring musician,' she says. 'I travel all over the place and I gig as performers do in Ireland.' Although she's not a session singer, Maura sometimes gets a call to 'guest' on other people's albums, such as Dolly Parton's most recent one, *Slow Dancing With The Moon*. The two singers are pictured together inside the CD sleeve, with a message from Maura which says: 'Dolly Parton is more than just a singer and writer. She's a modern day icon. Although I was as nervous as a child when I got to the studio, Dolly fixed me honey tea and made me feel right at home. She's indeed an incredible lady and a wonderful role model for all us girls in the music business.'

Maura points out: 'Generally speaking I'm not a session player because I'm not a perfect harmony singer. So I could never set myself up in the business. So, mostly, I just make records and tour. Where I'm very well known I play in theatres. Where I'm still building – because it's such a big country – I play in music clubs. Sometimes I open up the show for more established artistes. I've done a lot of work with John Prine. His audiences are a great mixture of people, from six to sixty. And when I go back to those venues in my own right, it's his audiences that come out to see me. Some weeks I do four-day weekends where I fly out to the shows. Sometimes, if I'm concentrating on an area, I might do two weeks, but not beyond that. I make my living from touring. It's not a luxury. I do from a hundred to a hundred and fifty dates a year.

'Everyone gets tired of life on the road. It's a tiring life. But there's drudgery in whatever life you have. When you're on the road, you wake up in the morning and you have to get from one city to the next. There's a day involved and then you get there, do the show, go to bed, get up and do it again. That is tiring. And it's tiring being up and positive and talking to people and being nice to everybody. That's as tiring as any travelling. Sometimes you get fed up of it and you want to be at home surrounded by your own stuff and talking to people that you know and who know you and who you don't have to explain yourself to. Every musician is faced with that. It's very stressful and it's very isolating and tiring and lonely, but at the same time it can be so much fun too. So, rather than stress the negative, you've got to stress the positive, because if you're home for any length of time and you're used to touring, then you just go crazy. I really love performing live. I get great pleasure from it. I'm not a writer, so performing and recording is the thing for me.'

Maura is signed to the 'alternative marketing department' of Warner Brothers. 'It means I'm not tied to any form or style,' she explains. 'I don't have to be a country singer, or I don't have to be a blues singer, or whatever. They are promoting me and marketing me as a singer. There are more and more people in the music business in that indefinable category – the one that really just means music. Because the industry is so big and because marketing strategies come from large numbers, they have now created a new category for us called "adult alternative", and that includes the likes of Lyle Lovett and k.d. lang. I'm not in their league by any means, yet. But that's where I'm headed, which is a very satisfying place to be musically.'

When she's selecting material for her albums, Maura says, 'I don't ever go for a particular direction in terms of song style. It's the song itself that creates the style. I go out looking for songs and finding them and liking them and going away from them and going back to them. Not necessarily because of a style, but because the song itself as a unit in each case was good. I've delved into all kinds of musical styles over the years in Nashville.' Finding songs, she told *The Irish Times*, 'is as simple and complicated as any art form. It's simple in that you know it when you find it. It's difficult because you can't describe it before you find it. My reaction when I find them is the same as anyone who hears a song that affects your heart and your soul.' Referring to one of her songs, 'I Would Be Stronger Than That', which is about a woman who is being abused, she says: 'There isn't one person who's heard that song who hasn't melted completely. When I was recording it, the sound engineer was so upset first time round, we had to do it again.'

That particular song drew an enthusiastic response from audiences on the *Woman's Heart* tours, featuring Maura, Dolores Keane, Frances Black and Eleanor McEvoy. They dedicated it to Lavinia Kerwick, the County Kilkenny rape victim who was devastated when she saw her attacker walk free from court with only a suspended prison sentence. 'That was very disheartening and disappointing for women. And maybe women need *A Woman's Heart* to feel that we are good. How can we say that women are doing well when we've got the Lavinia case and the X Case? But society in Ireland is changing. The doors are opening, I will say that. The curtains are being drawn back now and we know that there is no such thing as the perfect family. And I think that is a good thing because it will stop people pretending to themselves and hurting themselves and those around them. And I think it will be a way forward towards more freedom for everybody. There are situations, particularly abusive ones, where women have only seen that kind of reaction to women. Because there's a pattern of return in every relationship, if you think the way to go is to be beaten every night, then you won't think it's wrong when it happens to you. And you won't be inclined to talk about it.'

Maura accepts that society in Ireland is no longer afraid to discuss taboo subjects. People, both male and female, are openly discussing their personal and sexual affairs on radio chat shows like those of Gerry Ryan and Gay Byrne. 'When I was fourteen or fifteen or sixteen and not well versed in the ways of the world, the idea that anything explicit like that would be talked about on the radio or television would have embarrassed the hell out of me. But it would have been good to learn about stuff. *Jackie* magazine was the most explicit reading I had at that age. So it's now a more healthy environment. But, on the other hand, in America where I live, and I love being there, there seems to be a belief that telling your all to everybody will cure you. That's the other end of the spectrum.'

Maura stresses that she herself has never felt inferior as a woman. 'Both of my grandmothers were strong women. They were both widowed when they were young and left with large numbers of children and they were the role models for my mother and my father. And that was a role model that was given to me. There seems to be a backlash against feminism, but I wouldn't call myself a militant feminist because I don't need to be. I believe in myself and what I can do and was always given to believe in that. That's where freedom comes from. It's believing in yourself.'

She does not agree with some critics who have suggested that Eleanor McEvoy's song, 'Only A Woman's Heart', is sexist and anti-men, if only in its claim 'My heart is low, As only a woman's heart can be.' She told *Hot Press*: 'I've heard people say that this claim is anti-men, but that's not how I see it. My reading of the lyric is that Eleanor is talking hormonally, saying that women are naturally inclined towards sadness at least once a month. And the point is that women involve themselves and their emotions more in relationships than men do. Men won't get to the heart of their feelings because they are afraid of them. That's what I think Eleanor is talking about and I think she's right. I believe men don't know their sadness as much as women do. I'm not saying that all women are more in touch with their emotional life than all men. Certainly that's not true in relation to songwriters I use. Artistes are in tune with feelings we all share, irrespective of gender and that's exactly why I sing songs by men *and* women. Take "Feet Of A Dancer" [by Charlie McGettigan], I hope that when people hear that song they don't hear the man or the woman singing it, but the soul of the song. That's art to me. And I don't ever want to sing a song that doesn't have that core sense of truth and an appeal that crosses gender-lines.'

Maura married American Mac Bennett in April 1993. The couple met through friends and knew each other for two and a half years before they married. 'In Ireland that isn't very long, but in America it's an eternity,' she says. Mac works in the video business and he's also a writer and actor. Maura told *Hot Press*: 'A lot of people marry when they are very young and have no real experience of people or of love. I think there should be a law against that. I've had two or three extremely long relationships in my life and learned that, although there is an initial "in love" stage in a relationship, when everything is soft and romantic, that's not enough to build a life upon. The determining factor in love, for me, is learning to deal with those parts of a person's character that you don't even like. Any of us can fall in love with a romantic image of someone, most of us do to begin with. But you can't stay blind to their faults forever and it's only when you try to come to terms with all that, that you really know if you're in love or not. And too many people who go into marriage too young, get ready to leave as soon as romance dies. For me, love proves itself to be really mature when you realise you love a person who does make you cry, who can hurt you and whom you even hate sometimes.'

Their wedding in Ennis was, she says, 'great *craic*, mighty *craic*.' Mac was already familiar with Ireland. 'After we first met each other I did a tour here and he came over and travelled with us and hung about for awhile,' she explains. They live in what she describes as 'a ranch-style home' in Nashville. 'It's a very nice place that we bought last year [1992].' How does it compare to the area she grew up in? 'Well, it's a long way from the sea for a start. It's a very different living. But the people aren't all that different and that's the main thing. When the people from Arkansas and Tennessee came over to Ireland for our wedding, there was no strangeness between them and the people from Ireland. It was a wonderful thing to see.' As for having children, Maura told *Hot Press*: 'When I turned thirty I had a serious hormonal rush. It was really overwhelming and, in fact, I did seriously consider having a child at that point. But I talked to my sister and she said I was being very selfish and just feeding some notion out there in society. And she was right, to an extent. But, on the other hand, a woman does have to realistically face the fact that she is thirty. You look at your life and you realise what you have got left – eight, nine, ten years to have a child, if you're lucky. That is a reality you have to face. And I did at the time. I don't know if I could have children. There's no reason for thinking I couldn't. It's just the kind of paranoia that can hit a woman when you leave things a little late. I'd like to think that I can, but the reality is that I have a very hectic life and who knows if I can conceive or not. But I would be very disappointed and sad if I couldn't have a child.'

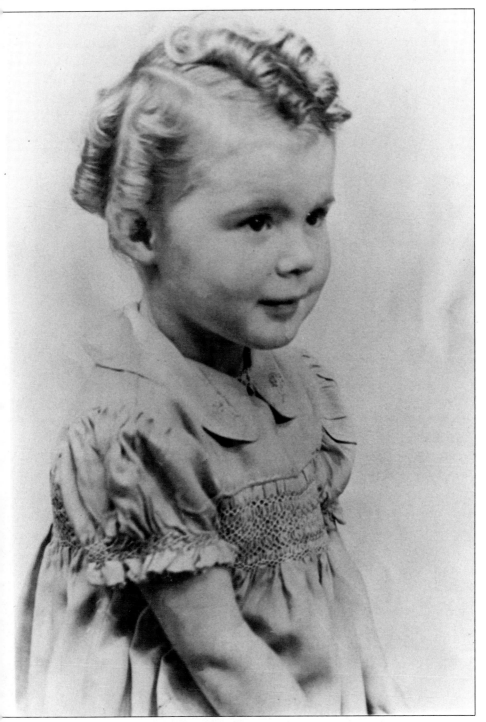

MAURA O'CONNELL AT ABOUT THREE YEARS OF AGE

ABOVE: Maura O'Connell on her First Communion day, with her sisters Aileen and Alisheen, and her father.

BELOW: Maura O'Connell on her father's knee, with her family in 1962. *Left to right*, Aileen, Amby (mother), Aine (baby), Alisheen, father and Maura.

ABOVE: Maura O'Connell in concert.
BELOW: Maura O'Connell (*second from right*) with her sisters.

ABOVE AND BELOW: MAURA O'CONNELL

ABOVE: Sharon Shannon (*left*) with her sisters Majella and Mary, July 1975. BELOW: The Shannon family. *Left to right*, Mary, Majella, Garry (in front with swan), father, Sharon.

TOP: Sharon Shannon on her mount Bouzouki at Ennis gymkhana, 1984.
LEFT: Sharon with kittens, 1984.
BELOW: Sharon with her pony, 1986.

ABOVE: Sharon Shannon in performance.
BELOW: Sharon playing at Ballyshannon with Arcady in 1988.

SHARON SHANNON

ABOVE: The Brennan family. *Back row, left to right,* Leo (father), Máire, Pól, Ciarán, Baba (mother). *Front row,* Deirdre, Enya, Leon.
BELOW: Máire's father Leo (*right*) with other family musicians; *left to right,* Uncle Lala, Gran Hardin, Aunt Rosemarie.

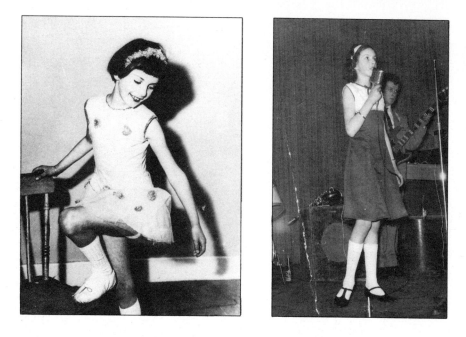

ABOVE, LEFT: Máire Brennan, about 1961. ABOVE, RIGHT: Máire performing with the Slieve Foy Band, 1965. BELOW: Máire's mother and father, Baba and Leo, in their pub, Leo's Tavern.

ABOVE: The Brennan parents playing with the Slieve Foy Dance Band. Leo (father) *centre*, and Baba (mother) *extreme right*. BELOW: CLANNAD – Pádraig, Pól, Ciarán, Enya, Noel, Máire.

ABOVE: Máire Brennan with her husband, the photographer Tim Jarvis.
BELOW: Máire signing albums in 1989.

ABOVE, LEFT: Mary Coughlan on her Confirmation day, aged eleven. ABOVE, RIGHT: The Coughlans. *Left to right*, Carol, Angela, Ger (*in front*) and Mary. BELOW: The Coughlan family. *Left to right*, father, Gerard, Angela, Carol, Mary, Martin with mother.

ABOVE, LEFT: Mary Coughlan on her First Communion day, 1962. ABOVE, RIGHT: Mary (*right*) with her sister Angela on her fourth birthday. BELOW: Mary Coughlan.

ABOVE AND BELOW: MARY COUGHLAN

MARY COUGHLAN WITH HER DAUGHTER CLARE, AT THE
NEIL YOUNG CONCERT IN SLANE.

SHARON SHANNON

SHARON SHANNON

Sharon Shannon is often regarded as an eccentric young woman because of her reluctance to give interviews to the press or to talk at length during a public performance. Others perceive her to be painfully shy and lacking in confidence. There may be a grain of truth in these assumptions. But one thing is certain, Sharon Shannon is an intelligent artiste who can mesmerise audiences with her musical skills. She is held in high esteem by the cream of the music world, having emerged as one of Ireland's most exciting and gifted musicians. Since her early days touring with The Waterboys, Sharon is now establishing her own profile around Europe as a solo performer. The summer of 1993 has been the most demanding in her short but eventful career. Her name featured on the bills of some of the biggest European festivals of the season.

In Ireland, Sharon became a household name when the country's most prestigious and longest-running TV chat show, *The Late Late Show*, devoted an entire programme to the celebration of her talent. Despite the plaudits from her peers, fans and the critics, Sharon remains endearingly unaffected and when she's not on tour it's not uncommon to find her in the middle of a *seisiún* in one of the pubs of Galway city where she now lives. There is no doubt that there is only one love in Sharon Shannon's life – music. When approached about this book, Sharon agreed to co-operate, but told her story through her friend, mentor, and manager, John Dunford.

Sharon comes from a farming background in Corofin, County

Clare, where her father I.J. specialised in raising horses. As a child, Sharon, who was born in 1968, developed a love for horses and I.J. and her mother, Mary, encouraged her to pursue her interest in showjumping. Her father maintains to this day that she would have made a major impression on the showjumping scene if she had continued that career. But Sharon dropped out of competitive showjumping when she was sixteen years old because her passion for music had taken over.

'My parents were always into music. They didn't play themselves, but they were set dancers and they always encouraged us to play. My older brother and sister, Gary and Majella, and my younger sister, Mary, and myself all learned to play the tin whistle. Gary was the one who got us all interested in music. When my mother and father realised that all of us were showing promise as musicians they decided to buy us each the musical instrument of our choice. I got a button accordion and that's how it all started for me. We taught ourselves to play. Teacher and musician Frank Custy, a family friend, also had a very big influence on me musically.' When he appeared on *The Late Late Show* tribute to Sharon, Frank Custy told Gay Byrne: 'I did very little with Sharon except encourage her. I think she was a genius from the word go. She loves what she's doing and I'm a great believer in enjoying your music. I'm not into competition. Music should be fun. Sharon proves that there is a love and enjoyment in her music.'

Her childhood years were idyllic, growing up on a farm in a happy family atmosphere. Her father worked hard on the land and with the horses. And while they weren't particularly affluent, their family circumstances were 'comfortable'. They never left the farm to go on holiday. 'We used to go to the beach and we went swimming in a lake near our home. But we couldn't leave the farm because there were cows to be milked and lots of other things to be looked after.' Sharon got involved in farm work and tending to the animals and grew up with a love of both the farm stock and nature in general. Emerging from this solid background, it's not surprising then to find that she has a very down-to-earth approach to her career. She became embroiled in the rich traditions of Irish music and dancing at a very early age. 'Our life was based around going to *seisiúns* and playing for set dancing. As a teenager, I never went to discos. I would go to a *céilí*.' All the Shannon children played in *Fleadh Ceoil*, but Sharon was never an All Ireland champion.' She was also involved in the Irish music organisation Comhaltas, and in her early teens she did two tours of the States with a group of traditional singers, musicians and dancers.

Sharon had no love for, nor interest in, the academic life, even though she was intelligent and did well in her exams. She went to secondary school at Colaiste Mhuire in Ennis, eight miles from her home in Corofin. Despite her abhorrence of the examination system, Sharon secured three honours in her Leaving Certificate and landed a place in University College Cork to pursue a degree in Arts. But she never adapted to university life. 'I had little time for college, so much so that I taught myself to play the fiddle during that period.' Sharon completed her first year, then packed it in. A secretarial course to learn shorthand and typing skills followed. Then she moved to Doolin in County Clare and played music with Mary Custy and Eoin O'Neill, a Dublin musician living there. While in Doolin, Sharon was approached by movie director Jim Sheridan, whose work includes *My Left Foot* and *The Field*. Jim asked Sharon to provide the music for the Druid Theatre's touring production of Brendan Behan's play, *The Hostage*. 'I toured Ireland with that and it was my first professional gig as a musician.'

Around that time, former De Danann supremo Johnny McDonagh was putting together a new group called Arcady. The group finally got up and running in 1987 with Frances Black as singer. Dolores Keane's brother, Seán, was also in the group, as was Cathal Hayden, now with the band Four Men And A

Dog. Johnny McDonagh then asked Sharon to join the outfit.

At the same time, John Dunford, who later became Sharon's manager and has played a major role in her career, was working as sound engineer and production manager with The Waterboys, then based in Spiddal. Johnny McDonagh contacted John and asked him to look after the sound for an Arcady gig in the Purty Loft in Dun Laoghaire, County Dublin. Dunford invited Mike Scott of The Waterboys to the show to see the band. Scott was completely enthralled by Sharon's music. Dunford says: 'Mike came to me after the show and said, "Jesus, she's fantastic. Wouldn't it be great if she was in the band?" Arcady weren't doing a lot of work on the live scene at that time, and Sharon had already told them she was leaving. John Dunford was putting together a small record label called Hummingbird with musician and broadcaster Philip King and John Kennedy, now U2's production manager. They decided to record Sharon Shannon. And so the famous Kinvara session of May 1989 was born. 'We set up in a pub for three days and invited people along to play on the album,' John Dunford remembers. 'Donal Lunny came along. So did Gerry O'Beirne, who is now in her band. Adam Clayton [from U2] came down from Dublin. Mike Scott came over with Steve Wickham, also from The Waterboys. It was at that stage Mike came to me and said, "I've made up my mind. I'm going to ask Sharon to join the band."'

Sharon Shannon joined The Waterboys on her twenty-first birthday in June 1989 and went on to work with them on a major tour around the world. Among other shows in Britain, Sharon performed with the group at the Glastonbury Festival, she then toured with them in Europe and America. The band worked from June until Christmas of that year and went on to record another album in Spiddal, which took them through to September 1990. At that stage, Steve Wickham decided to leave the group. Mike Scott felt that Steve united the rock element of the band with the traditional side – Sharon. So, after a meeting, The

Waterboys decided to split up. 'My time with The Waterboys was great because I was introduced to different types of music and I was working on rock shows. Now, I'm as comfortable doing a festival as I am a smaller show.' During her time with The Waterboys, Sharon established a strong bond of friendship with the individual members and she remembers well the day they all dropped into her parents' home for a major session that went on for about nine hours.

Sharon still hadn't completed her solo album by the time she parted company with The Waterboys, so she asked John Dunford to produce it for her. She had no record deal and no management at that stage, so John also took over those responsibilities. 'We worked together. There was no real plan. We said we'd give it a try and see how it went for a year,' Sharon recalls. The album, *Sharon Shannon*, was released to critical acclaim and enjoyed healthy sales. Then Sharon was invited to feature on the 1992 album, *A Woman's Heart*, and her solo career suddenly took off. It was at Christmas that year that *The Late Late Show* decided to build a special programme around her. They had done similar shows on The Chieftains and The Dubliners. And they were keen to give a rising young performer a break. Sharon fitted the bill. A host of top musicians, including her colleagues on the album *A Woman's Heart*, and Adam Clayton, Mike Scott and Liam O'Maonlai from The Hothouse Flowers, turned up to pay tribute to her. The show was hugely popular with the TV audience and has now been released on video. One of the most remarkable aspects of the night is that Sharon won over the studio audience and the viewers with few words, allowing her music to speak for itself. On the question of interviews with the media, Sharon confesses: 'I feel really uncomfortable with them.'

Success brings its own pressures, and a hectic touring schedule can take a musician away from home for months at a time. But Sharon is determined to work on her own terms. She enjoys being at home and will spend a maximum of two and a half weeks away on tour. 'I wouldn't like to go off for six weeks or two months. I'd stop enjoying it and it would become a chore.' She also likes to spend as much time as possible listening to new music and going to see other people perform. 'I need to take time out to soak up music and while I'm working there isn't time to do that. I need to hear things and get ideas. I listen to music in my home and I travel to hear people. Galway and Clare are fantastic for that.' Sharon's musical influences spread outside the general area of Irish traditional music. 'I'm very influenced by Cape Breton and French Canadian music. A lot of Irish and Scottish people moved to the Cape Breton isles around the Famine time and there's a really different tradition of music there. It's a cross between Irish, Scottish, Cajun and country. I love Scottish music and Shetland tunes in particular. I have to love a piece of music myself before I'll entertain the idea of playing it. I have begun to write myself. It's coming along. I like modern arrangements. I love bass drums and piano. In my current band, I have bass guitar and fiddle. It's a tight unit. Máire Breathnach, who is in the band, writes all the time and we play her tunes in the set. Gerry O'Beirne, who is also in the band, has written for me as well. And Steve Cooney has written a lot of stuff that we use.'

Although she also plays the fiddle, Sharon is mainly identified with the button accordion. 'The one I'm playing at the moment is an Italian model, a Castagnari. The people who make it run a small family business that has been going for three hundred years. I don't think there are many musicians in Ireland playing them. I also play a French accordion, a Salturelle which is a favourite with many Irish musicians.'

Sharon is not motivated by the desire to amass her own crock of gold. Neither is she turned on by the idea of being a personality, a famous person. None of the attention she has been subjected to so far in her short career has affected her because she doesn't see herself as someone special. 'That's another reason why she doesn't like doing interviews, because she just sees herself as a normal person,' says John Dunford. 'She's thankful and honoured that people come to her gigs and people buy her album, but she doesn't feel that she's anything exceptional – and she's embarrassed by people who think she is.' Whatever money she has earned from her music has been invested in her own semi-detached house at Taylor's Hill in Galway. 'Shopping is another of my greatest pleasures in life, and I enjoy shopping for antiques and furniture. In my spare time, I also like making my own clothes and I've made curtains for the house. I love cooking and trying out different dishes. When I'm at home you'll also find me pottering around in the garden because that's one of my favourite hobbies. I do a good bit of swimming in the sea. But playing music tops everything that I love. And I like playing with lots of different people, whether it's on a professional level or just for enjoyment at sessions in the local pubs. I like watching movies and I love the theatre. Galway is great for that and I go to see a lot of theatre things there. One of my favourite events of the year is the Galway Arts Festival. I love the carnival atmosphere surrounding that event.'

Although she has made a major impact on the Irish scene, Sharon Shannon's career on the international circuit is still in its infancy, but it is growing all the time. 'The festivals in Europe are now getting better and better. The requests for Sharon to do festivals are getting bigger. Sharon is getting a higher profile in Europe all the time,' John Dunford confirms. 'There's a network of festivals there and if you do one it has a domino effect on the rest of them. There was one festival in Europe last year where Sharon was lined up in the early stages and they put her photograph on the cover of the programme. That resulted in us getting four festivals out there this year. So, touring in Europe is now starting to pay its way. It's very difficult to make money out of touring. When you add up the cost of paying a band, transport, sound equipment, lights, hotels and stuff, you really don't make that much money. We did four tours in America in the last two years and they have all cost money to do. We take money from the live work in Ireland to pay for the American tours. The Irish dates always subsidised the American tours and the European tours. But now that we are moving up the bill at shows and doing more and more work abroad, the foreign touring is beginning to pay for itself.'

MÁIRE BRENNAN

MÁIRE BRENNAN

Life has never been so good for Máire Brennan. Her career with family group Clannad is healthier than ever. And in tandem with her career, her personal life has knitted together in a dream-like pattern. Married for the second time at thirty-nine, she became pregnant almost immediately and gave birth to daughter Aisling, now aged two. And, at the time of writing, Máire was expecting her second child. The children have come along at a stage when her work commitments are greater than they have ever been in the twenty years since the group first recorded. Clannad's 1993 album, *Banba*, has created a huge demand for the group in Britain. And America is opening up for them as a result of one of their numbers, 'Theme From Harry's Game', being featured on a US Volkswagen TV advertisement.

But Máire is determined to balance a career and motherhood. 'Just when I thought I'd got to a certain stage of my life, here is more coming,' Máire says, reflecting on her current position in the music scene. 'I can't believe it. I'm really enjoying all the stuff that's happening around me at the moment. It's brilliant after twenty years to feel that there's still so much out there for you to achieve. Lots of women seem to be able to combine motherhood and a career in the music business and do it quite well. It doesn't have that stigma attached to it that it used to. Look at Chrissie Hynde, Annie Lennox and Mary Black. It hasn't been a problem for Mary at all. She has been brilliant. But I feel very fortunate that Tim, my husband, gives me such support.

Sometimes children, when they are young, can adapt to the way you are, rather than you adapting to them. I think it's better to go ahead and have a child if you want to, rather than waiting for whatever stage of your career to pass over. Things will fall into place around it. I'm a great believer in that. Anyway, I feel really fortunate to be able to have children.

'Children can dictate a certain amount in your life, which I don't mind at all. But it is tougher on women, especially if you have to leave your children behind for the odd week here and there. It's difficult, of course it is. It's always been accepted that men go out and earn the crust. So if they have to go away for a week or whatever, it's automatically accepted. Next year we're touring Australia, New Zealand and certain parts of Europe. I'll be a mum on the road with a family. I'm looking forward to it. Why not? There are so many things that you can arrange on the road now. You can have a caterer and there's a company that organises backstage crèches in various cities. So there's so much more available for the likes of myself in that situation. The rock 'n' roll scene has changed in that respect. I think it's a sign of people getting their priorities right. It's nice to be able to enjoy being on tour and still be part of a family, rather than going away and finding your family half-grown by the time you come off the road. That's what has happened to a lot of people in the rock 'n' roll business.'

Throughout her career, Máire – pronounced Moya – has displayed a determination and strength of character that has taken her through many a bleak phase both professionally and in her private life. Although surrounded by a group of family members, she has had to summon up every ounce of will power to pull her through the troubled spots. Máire has proven that everyone can eventually make a success of their life and career using a combination of self-belief, dogged determination and sheer hard work, with the emphasis on the latter. Her survival and the survival of Clannad in the precarious showbiz world can almost certainly be attributed to their roots in the bleak but beautiful craggy terrain around Gweedore in north west Donegal. Clannad are a phenomenon on the Irish music scene, just for their staying-power alone. But they always had a solid, down-to-earth approach to their work, never striving for instant success. 'Like Mary Black, Dolores Keane and Maura O'Connell, we've been putting in the years. It's a case of getting out there, sticking with it, really believing in what you do and doing it well. It certainly isn't an overnight thing,' Máire explained in a special interview for this book.

People are always surprised to learn that Máire Brennan was born in Dublin and lived there until she was two and a half years old. Her parents, Leo and Baba Brennan, eloped to Dublin because Máire's maternal grandparents were opposed to them marrying. 'My mum was a schoolmaster's daughter and my father was a musician at the time, so he wasn't perceived to be good husband material. They eloped during Lent, a period when there were no dances. They were in their early twenties and as soon as they married my father was totally accepted into my mother's family.' Leo and Baba – her real name is also Máire – stayed on in Dublin for a while and both Máire and her brother, Ciaran, were born there. 'I don't remember being in Dublin,' Máire says, 'but I remember the train journey back to Donegal. I remember being fascinated with the train.'

There is a history of music in her family, stretching back through generations. 'My father's family came from the music world. My grandfather and grandmother had a band. She was the drummer in it. My father and his brothers and a sister were also part of it. They had a sort of travelling roadshow and went all over Ireland, setting up in a town for a week and putting on a variety show which had acrobatics and gags as well as music. My dad would come out with the accordion and play a couple of tunes. Before the last couple of shows my grandfather would cycle on to the next town thirty miles away and get the hall sorted out for the next performance. There were a couple of families who had that kind of show on the road. It later developed into a showband, which was called The Slieve Foy, after the mountain in Carlingford. It was my grandfather's life and he died doing what he loved. He suffered a heart attack playing on stage at a dance one night. As he was being carried away by my uncle, he said, "Play on, the audience comes first." Those were the last words my father heard him say.'

The Slieve Foy was a mixture of *céilí* and Glen Miller and her father later became leader of the band. 'They always played Glasgow on St Patrick's Day and I remember one time I went with them. I was into Irish dancing, but I was also into the charts. I got up on stage with them and sang "My Boy Lollipop" in my Irish step-dancing outfit. I was eleven years of age,' Máire recalls. 'Being a drummer way back then and even to this day was very unusual for a woman, but my grandmother was a very independent woman. I must have got something from her. She was English and she used to say that her grandmother was a French pianist. So there's music along the line for a long time.

'On my mother's side, my grandparents, Hughie and Mary Duggan, taught me at primary school. It was a great national school. We did a lot more than learning the normal subjects. We also had music and art in the school. And my grandfather used to tell us a story a week from Greek mythology. During the summer there was a travelling singer and musician who used to call to the school. We used to sit and listen to him telling stories and singing songs for two hours. My grandfather thought it was so educational. I thought so as well. It was all a great introduction to creative thinking.' Máire remembers spending a lot of the summer digging turf in the bog for the winter fuel. 'It was a major thing. All the families around did it.' She also remembers fishing in the streams with homemade rods. 'They were the tastiest fish you'd ever eat.'

Christmas was a special time in the Gaeltacht where she grew up. 'We used to put on the only Irish pantomime that existed in Ireland. It was written by great local people and it was based on mythical stories. November to January was completely occupied by pantomime. I started very young because I was in the fairy scene first and then I became the queen and then I was principal girl. Buses would come from Belfast and Dublin especially for it because it was in Gaelic.' The Brennan family stood out as talented singers, musicians and dancers from an early age, taking part in local *feiseanna* and scooping the top prizes. 'I never knew music to be something I learned. It was always normal for me to be singing or dancing,' Máire says. Around the age of nine, Máire took an interest in ballet. She recalls how she used to buy the *Bunty* and *Judy* magazines 'to see the [ballet] steps they had in it. My father used to take me out to Derry every second Saturday for an hour's lesson because I insisted I wanted to learn ballet. It must have been horrendous for him because it was a two-hour drive both ways.'

When the time came for Máire to move on to secondary school, she was sent to boarding school at the Ursuline Convent in Sligo. 'My father sent me there because he thought it would be really nice for me to learn the harp and he knew they taught the harp in Sligo. The Ursulines had a very good name for music. They had choirs and everything. I hated the harp at first because I hated the image of a girl singing with the harp. My father had such a burning passion for music that when his own group disbanded twenty-four years ago he bought a pub in Gweedore as an outlet for his music. He never drank nor smoked in his life, so he was an unusual man to own a pub. But he bought it for music, so that he could entertain in it. The only thing my father ever knew was music and he didn't want to be going around just playing at weddings and cabarets. So he bought a pub and turned it into a musical lounge and it became a stage for us. When I came home for my holidays from boarding school, I used to refuse to get up and play the harp and sing. I was just into singing with the boys.' Máire was thirteen when she first went to boarding school, and at first she found the system quite difficult because until then she had studied all her subjects through Irish. But while it was a culture shock, she soon adapted. 'I think it did me the world of good because I came from a remote area and I made new friends. And as regards music, it was brilliant because they had operas and things like that.'

At school in Sligo, Máire became something of a celebrity when she started appearing on TV after winning a major competition with her brothers Ciaran and Pól, and uncles Noel and Pádraig Duggan – the original Clannad line-up. 'When we used to play in my father's pub during the summer, we didn't have a name. I wouldn't be on stage with them all the time. They would be doing Donovan and Dylan. But if they were doing The Beach Boys or The Mamas And Papas I'd get up with them and then I'd do a Joni Mitchell song. The boys won the Slógadh competition at the beginning of 1970 and afterwards the local garda sergeant came in with an entry form for the Letterkenny Folk Festival. We were debating among ourselves about entering right up to the final date for entry. We could see the mail van coming in the distance and with minutes to spare we decided to have a go. But what would we call ourselves? Somebody suggested *Clann As Dobhar* [a family from Dobhar], but everyone thought that was a bit of a mouthful. Then it was suggested: "Why don't we just take the 'a' and the 'd' and just stick it on to *Clann*?" And that's the name that stuck.

In the Letterkenny competition you had eight minutes to do whatever you wanted. At that stage I wasn't doing anything on the harp with the boys, but they suggested I should include it. Outside of hymns, the only other thing I knew on the harp was "Brian Boru's March". But I used to play it slow. So I started to play that and the boys started to arrange around me – Pól on the bongos, Ciaran on the electric bass and so on. Then they suggested I should be the main vocal and sing the song that Noel was going to sing, a local Gaelic song, and they did the harmony to it. We felt we should also do an English song. But we didn't have a folk song in English. A friend came up with "Kitty of Coleraine", which was far removed from anything we ever did. It was awful. But we went out and won and it was one of the most magical moments of my life. I'll never forget it. We had been up against tough competition: the McGlynns of Sligo, who had just signed a major recording contract with CBS; the Connollys from Galway; and the Sands from Newry. One of the judges, Tony McCawley from BBC Northern Ireland, said he was floored by us. He wasn't expecting a band to come out and have such variety in their eight minutes.'

Their prize was a recording contract with Polygram, but it took them three years to get it recorded because the record company felt that an album of Gaelic songs would never sell. In the meantime, Máire returned to boarding school in Sligo. 'Any Irish shows that were on TV used to ask us to come and perform. So Ciaran, who was in Gweedore, used to set about getting some of the old songs my grandparents would have. Pól was in boarding school in Sligo as well and he would send us on our parts and the words. The day before we were due in RTE, Ciaran and my mother would collect myself and Pól from school and we'd meet Pádraig and Noel who were training as radio officers at Bolton Street College in Dublin. We'd rehearse a brand new song that night and go on and record it for TV the following day. And, on the night it was on, the whole school would sit around the television and watch the programme and there'd be a big cheer at the end.'

In 1973, Clannad took part in the National Song Contest, singing a Gaelic song, 'An Phairc', written by Mick Hanley. Because of the publicity and prestige surrounding their participation in the TV contest, Polygram decided it was an opportune time to record the album which Clannad had been promised. Máire recalled how one of the exciting moments during the recording of the album [*Clannad*] was the arrival in the studio of Shay Healy. 'He was writing for *Spotlight* magazine at the time and I was completely in awe of him. *Spotlight* was a sort of bible to teenagers at the time and for Shay Healy to be interested in what we were doing was exciting.' Despite the release of the album, Clannad didn't turn professional until 1976.

After completing her Leaving Certificate, Máire spent a year in Gweedore working in the bar. She then went to the Royal Irish Academy of Music for a couple of years, with a view to teaching music, and studied the concert harp, which is different to the Irish harp. Máire landed a job teaching in a boys' secondary school in Falcarragh, twelve miles from her home in Gweedore. 'All during this time we'd be asked to do TV shows. Gael Linn also got interested in us and asked us to do another album, which was great because we got to do as many Gaelic songs as we wanted. But we still didn't think of it professionally. It was only when we met a German couple, who came looking for us after they had heard one of our albums, that the turning point came. They ran thirty or forty folk festivals around Germany every year and they asked us over. At that stage I was teaching in Falcarragh, so I had to take time off. We did thirty or thirty-five concerts and the last one was in the Berlin Philharmonic Hall. We were the last act on and we got a standing ovation. So we went into the dressing room and took a look at each other and said, "Well, will we go professional or what?" My two uncles had just qualified as radio officers to go off on the ships, but we said we might as well give it a go for a couple of years. We still say that to this day. People in Ireland thought we were crazy because they said, "You'll never get anywhere singing Gaelic songs."

'We did six albums before anything major happened to us.

But we were quite happy going to Europe twice a year and doing major shows and doing a tour in Ireland. We weren't able to play in the pubs in Ireland because there was a huge ballad boom at the time. So we used to write to all the convents and colleges and secondary schools and offer to play during the daytime. If there was twenty pence on the door and six hundred kids, it was a good door. Often we'd arrive at a convent and the nun would say, "I'm really sorry, I've only got fifty names." It was only when they saw the transit van pulling up and a guy with long hair getting out, real cool dudes, that they changed their minds. By the time the boys had the speakers set up, everybody in the school was going. I still meet up with people who remember us from the schools.' Looking back on her role as a woman in a band in the late seventies, Máire says it was in no way subservient to the lads. 'I knew how to put up speakers and microphones and I still do. Sometimes I had to do it all. I was also the main money person. I was called "Moneybag" because I looked after the financial end of things. I was definitely one of the lads on the road. That's why I'm such a sports person. When you travel around with a bunch of guys who are into sport you might as well join them. I got into watching sport with them, so much so that I'm probably worse than they are now. Being a family, it wasn't such a big deal for me to go into the boys' room and sprawl across a bed to watch TV. If they had just been friends it might have been different.

'The early days on the road were exciting and I didn't think it was tough at the time. I remember heading up to Hamburg and there was ice inside the transit van. I recall being caught in the snow loads of times or the times when the transit van would break down when you'd be trying to make it to a gig. Looking back it was tough, but they are the things that harden you. But it's good for you to go through that because you appreciate things later in life. Now I appreciate the smallest things that happen to me. I still get a buzz from lots and lots of things and I think that's the reason.

It's a tough life but you have to adapt to it.'

Their career took off in 1982 when they wrote the theme song for *Harry's Game*, a TV thriller about Northern Ireland. Clannad entered the British Top 20 for the first time, where the single reached number five. Suddenly they were fashionable and won over a whole new audience. Clannad's music is inspired by the wonderful area where they were reared. Gweedore and surrounding districts are steeped in folklore and tradition. Máire's uncle, Padraig Duggan, told *The Sunday World* how they used to 'go round with a tape-recorder taping the auld ones singing songs. We'd go to Tory Island and talk to old people ... We were related to some of them as well.' And they developed their own distinctive sound by arranging old traditional songs. 'We got it from beautiful melodies – lovely words and airs,' Máire says. 'Our songs are in the place where we come from, but it's something I can't describe,' she once told *The Irish Times*. 'There's no explaining it. The only way to explain it is to say "Come up to Gweedore." It's full of stories. Every hill has a tale people tell about it.'

In another interview she said that their sound came from both sides of the family. 'We used what was in both families. Dad played at *céilís* when that gig was going, but basically he used to play clarinet and saxophone. My mother's side was the poetry books and books of songs. But it's only when you start talking to people about the what, why and when of Clannad that you realise how much of Gweedore is in the songs. When you bring people up who mightn't be interested in us or even never heard that much and take them to Gweedore, then they immediately understand the band.' Speaking to *The Daily Mail*, Máire said: 'I think people who listen to us like to relax and let their minds wander. My voice is very soulful. I'm an extremely romantic, passionate person – anything at all and I'm in tears.' She told Joe Jackson in *Hot Press* that Clannad should be 'viewed within the tradition of songwriters who use words primarily to evoke images, colours, shades of dark and light and who are, in essence, more soundscape painters than songwriters.'

Máire has never been noted for expressing strong political views or for commenting on social issues. 'We've always steered clear of making political statements and preferred to represent the beauty and cultural side of Ireland,' she told *The Daily Mail.* 'Today, being proud of your country only gets you into trouble. I have no time for killing at all. I don't care what it is. There are always people who will support the IRA, or they wouldn't get away with it. But, in general, Irish people are sick of them, particularly after what happened in Warrington. My heart just bled for those dead children.

'Clannad don't want to be political because, I think, music can carry so much. I like to think music can heal wounds. I was brought up in Donegal and both sides used to come down here for holidays and it's so sad that that hardly happens anymore. I've married a Protestant man and, because I'm a Catholic, we call ourselves Christians. We felt one always looks at the differences rather than the similarities.' She suggested in *Hot Press* that the situation in Northern Ireland is 'a central sorrow' in the lives of all Irish people. 'It was that feeling that we tried to evoke in "Harry's Game". I honestly believe that music is a unifying factor, politically. For the rest of my life I'll always remember singing that song in Belfast and being overcome by this truly magical and healing feeling of unity. Because we sing Gaelic songs it's often said, "Oh, you must be on that side." But the song isn't for one side or against the other. It's an evocation of the hopelessness that everyone must feel about what's happening in the North. But, again, we really do prefer to leave a question mark hanging in the air after our songs, rather than offering false solutions – especially in relation to the North, where too many people sit down and talk or write or sing in ways that offer useless, superficial readings of the situation. And equally superficial solutions.'

Along her musical route, Máire did a duet with Bono of U2 – 'In A Lifetime' from Clannad's 1986 album, *Macalla*. The song was released as a single and took her into the British Top 20. Her sister, Enya, was also a member of Clannad during the early stages of her career. But she left and became a recording artiste in the superstar league. At the time Enya said she felt that she wasn't being accepted as an equal. Máire later told *The Sunday World*: 'Enya joined us at the end of 1979. At that stage the rest of the band knew each other inside out. It would have been difficult for anybody to come into a band like us, a family, even though she was family. She was just out of college. She had done a lot more classical music and just wanted to develop a lot more different things. I'm sure it did her the world of good being with us for the couple of years. When she did want to go her own way she had our complete blessing. She's my sister and I love her a lot.'

In 1992, Máire achieved a personal musical ambition by releasing a solo album. She was pregnant with Aisling while working on the album and she admits: 'I seemed to have got off on being happy. I had expected to write a couple of numbers and then search for new material. But to my amazement I kept on writing and writing and it turned out really well. My confidence just seemed to soar. It was a challenge, but I wasn't afraid of it. I just went for it. It did extremely well for me, selling two hundred thousand copies, and it's doing well for me in America. There's no way I expected that, so I was thrilled to bits. It was something I wanted to do for a long time and it was in me to do and you never know what else I might come up with. People respected me for it and were happy with the outcome of it. It wasn't the big flop that some people thought it might be. I only brought it out for my own satisfaction. I wanted to do it and see how it would turn out.'

In her personal life, Máire went through the pain of a failed marriage to a Dublin musician she married in 1983. 'We had been going out for six years before we got married, but unfortunately the marriage only lasted for twenty-one months. Fortunately, we didn't have kids. It was at a time when "Harry's Game" had happened and it was a busy time in Clannad. I was doing more work than we had been used to. It's difficult being married to a musician anyway. You really need somebody to understand you and be behind you. And if somebody else is in the same business, sometimes it doesn't work out like that. The decision to part was mutual in the end.' Máire admits the break-up had a devastating effect on her: 'I was very disgusted with myself. I felt very low. I was very depressed and I didn't know where I was going or what I was doing. I was in Nowhere Land for a year or so. You start putting yourself down. You blame yourself and it gets worse and worse. You try to drown your sorrows and that makes it ten times worse. I'm sure a lot of people go through that. It leaves its scars.'

But Máire's life took a new turn six years ago when a journalist and a photographer from the British music magazine *New Musical Express* (NME) arrived in Gweedore to do a feature on Clannad, following the release of their album, *Sirius*. Máire recalls having 'a brilliant day' with writer Alan Jackson and photographer Tim Jarvis. 'We showed them all round the place, brought them up to Leo's and the local disco and we dropped them back to their hotel at about five o'clock in the morning. I didn't see them the next morning before they left, but I got a gorgeous letter from Tim two weeks later. He said how much he was taken with me and the place. I was taken with him as well. We both were without acknowledging it at the time. So we arranged to meet in London and it's been going ever since. He was living in London and I was in Dublin, so it was a good test if something was going to work out. We never lived together before we married. We are both strong Christians and we had both become so before we met. I needed something in my life more than music and I had gone back to my religion and to reading a bit more into it.' The couple married in January 1991 at a quiet family ceremony in Cambridge. 'I was lucky that I fell for an Englishman,' she says. 'If it was an Irishman I don't know what the situation would have been. I suppose live together like a lot of people do.' Although Máire loves Ireland and feels it's a better society for rearing children, she says: 'If there are any faults in the Irish people it's the way we tend to sweep things like marriage breakdown under the carpet.'

On the question of her financial status, Máire readily admits that people assume she's in the millionaire bracket. 'People think I'm loaded, but I'm not,' she says. 'It's probably our own fault, the fact that we haven't made multi-millions. Sometimes we've been naive enough to spend too much money doing an album, and a record company is only a bank. I rent a house in Dublin. I don't own a car. I have a little bungalow in Donegal, but I haven't got property all over the place. Overall, the albums have sold a lot. But individually we haven't sold a million of any one album and that's where it counts. A lot of money goes into recording and promoting each album and it has to be paid back to the record company.' Material gain has never been the driving force in Máire's career. Máire and Clannad haven't earned a significant amount of cash in their long-running career. 'It doesn't bother me having been in the business for so long and not having made enough [money] out of it,' Máire told *The Sunday World*. 'I have a good life and I do consider myself lucky. I'm not materialistic. I don't think Irish people in general are materialistic. You can't buy happiness no matter how much money you have. I'd much rather be in this situation and be as happy and content as I feel. I'm quite positive about myself now.' She told *The Daily Mail*: 'We're successful but not in a high-powered, high-pressured way. I'm so glad I'm not in Bono's shoes because I wouldn't want my career to take over my whole life. I still get so much joy from something like our latest album [*Banba*] going straight into the British charts at number five. I'm still recording after twenty years, but I haven't killed myself for twenty years. We've survived because we were never determined to become rich and famous. We enjoyed making the music so much and we were just surprised when we found we were getting paid for it.'

Máire has long since left her wild days on the road behind her. 'I downed many a vodka,' she says, looking back on her career. 'Now I don't drink spirits at all. I think everyone goes through a period where you take on life and you think you can do everything. You go nightclubbing. You stay out 'till the morning. You do all those things and you get up the next morning and wonder why you did it. Then you say, "Never again." And what do you do? You go out and do it all over again. You think you're out having a good time, but you end up more depressed than anything. You have to have a reasonable life to make sense of it and part of it is being with somebody you love and having a good relationship. That kind of thing is really important and when you have that, things like drinking and staying out all night are not so important. When you're in a happy relationship, you can enjoy life doing simple things, like going down to the beach for a walk or going for a drive in the countryside.'

Máire feels that it's a good time for women to make their mark in Ireland. 'It seems to be the right time for it and people are going for it. The *Woman's Heart* album is phenomenal. It's a great album. It set a great standard for women singers and musicians around Ireland. It was absolutely wonderful and people are into good music and good songs from women. It has shown that there are a lot of strong women out there determined to have careers and going for it and people like what they are doing.'

MARY COUGHLAN

MARY COUGHLAN

Galway-born singer Mary Coughlan engenders a volcanic rage in some Irish people with her no-holds-barred criticism of Irish society in general and the Catholic Church in particular. Her razor-sharp tongue and colourful language send faint-hearted souls scurrying for cover. But peel back the outer layer from this gutsy lady and underneath is a sensitive, compassionate, loving human being who has been dealt more than her fair share of blows in life. When Mary Coughlan sings the blues, it's from the heart. She has been there. But she has also embraced life with the enthusiasm of a hound in pursuit of its prey. She has enjoyed its pleasures as well as its pains. Her story is full of bizarre twists and turns that have taken her from obscurity to celebrity status as a singer – only to see it all collapse around her like a house of cards. She lost one home and bounced back, only to see the same nightmare scenario starting all over again. And always hanging over her was the threat that a drink problem would send her plunging into the depths of society's sewers. If there is one sin that Mary Coughlan is guilty of perhaps, it's of being her own worst enemy in many respects. She has never taken the easy road in her private life, or played the showbiz games by cultivating the type of image that would give her a smooth passage in the popularity stakes. But she has proven herself to be a survivor both off-stage and in the public domain as a performer.

Her father Peter Doherty, a soldier, is a native of Burnfoot, County Donegal, while her mother, Peggy Cooke, came from

Cillchiaráin, Connemara, County Galway. Born and reared in Galway where she grew up in the Shantalla housing estate, Mary recalls how every summer the Coughlan kids would be packed off to Burnfoot for their holidays.

'We'd all go up, but my father would have to go back to work after two weeks and we were left up there with my grannie and grandfather, Maggie and Pat Doherty. Daddy had two brothers and a sister living in Scotland and their kids would come over as well, so we had a ball. It was a small farmhouse and there would be as many as twelve or thirteen of us in the same bedroom, sleeping on mattresses on the floor. We used to stick pins into each other and we rarely slept as far as I can recall. My grandparents had chickens and they'd slaughter one every Friday or Saturday for the Sunday dinner and we'd have boiled eggs every morning for breakfast. The house was down a boreen, about a mile and a half from the main Letterkenny/Derry road, so it was fairly remote. A Protestant family, the Ramseys, lived next door and there were no other people around for miles.

'Like most rural houses at that time, there was no water on tap and my grandmother had to walk quite a distance for water. She'd fill two buckets at a time and carry them home balanced on a broomstick across her shoulders. We'd all be sent to the well for water and we used to love it. I can still remember that time and place with great fondness. Although we spent Christmas Day at home, we used to go up to Donegal around the Christmas period as well. Winters are quite harsh up there and we got snowed in one time at the Gap of Dungloe. It was a long drive to Burnfoot, which is about one hundred and eighty miles from Galway. We travelled by car. I think my father was one of the first people on the street to have a car.'

Mary's early childhood was a happy, carefree time. But war broke out with her soldier father as soon as she reached adolescence. 'I'm the eldest of five and when I reached the age of thirteen things started to tighten up at home as regards my freedom and I wasn't one to be tightened up. So I started to rebel and there was murder in our house on a daily basis. I became a hippy and I began wearing bell-bottom trousers, huge elephant flares with Ban the Bomb signs on them. I had an old army bag with dollies tied out of them and Peace signs. In one fit of rage my father took it and burnt it. I got a job that summer in a local supermarket where I was earning four pounds a week. But I had to be home at ten o'clock every night or my father would come looking for me. There were certain people I wasn't allowed to hang out with because they would be a bad influence on me. But sure I was as bad as any of them. I was allowed to the hops [discos] in the local Hangar ballroom, which were non-alcoholic. But there were certain things I wasn't allowed to go to, so I had to sneak out through my bedroom window at night to attend them. I went to see Donovan, and Planxty, who were playing support to him. My father was waiting outside the hall for me and when I came out he disgraced me in front of my friends. Another night I went to see the group Taste in the Hangar and he came in and took me out of it. I was mortified.'

By this stage, Mary had moved on to secondary school in the local Presentation Convent. But very soon she was establishing a reputation as a troublemaker. 'I hated the nuns and I began running away from home and school on a regular basis. My parents were driven up the wall with me. On one occasion when I mitched from school with some friends, we took boats from the boating club and we rowed up the Corrib [lake] and stayed overnight on an island. I was only fourteen years old at the time and my parents had the Guards and everyone out looking for us. At school, I hated having to wear a uniform and I would deliberately antagonise the nuns by wearing yellow socks when I was supposed to wear brown. I'd be sent home with a note to change them. Sometimes I didn't go home or if I

did my mother would make me put on brown socks, but I'd slip
a pair of purple ones in my bag and put them on before going
back into school again. I used to ask the nuns awkward questions about why the bishop was driving a big fancy car and why
they had so much money. I delighted in doing things like that,
which they hated. The bishop at the time was Dr Michael Brown
and he lived in a big palace up at Taylor's Hill. We used to raid
apples in his orchard and I could never understand why he had
such a big fancy house – I think there were twenty-eight
bedrooms in it. It was the most beautiful place surrounded by
walls.'

Mary stopped going to church when she was thirteen and she
remembers how she used to spend Sunday afternoons drinking
booze in a derelict house with a gang of friends. 'One of the
lads would liberate a car from his parents while they were at
Mass and we'd liberate a barrel of booze from outside a pub in
Galway. We'd take it up to a derelict house in Salthill, open it
with a screwdriver and hammer and hold a saucepan under it
to collect the booze. There were ten or fifteen of us and we'd
demolish the barrel before we came home. I suppose we'd only
have two or three pints each by the time everyone got one. I
rarely went to school and I was expelled before my Inter Cert
for giving abuse to teachers, mitching and running away. They
allowed me to sit the exam and although I got five honours, they
wouldn't have me back. My mother went down to them and
begged and pleaded, to no avail. My mother then traipsed
around all the schools in town. I had a terrible reputation and
Galway is a small city. Apart from the Presentation, there were
only the Mercy and Dominican convents and they knew all
about me. I was eventually taken into the Dominican College
after promising to be good – down on my knees in front of the
Reverend Mother. There was a little chapel in the school and
she put me in there and told me to think about my future and
what I was doing to my family. Then she locked the door and

left me there for an hour. I just sat there bored. But I said I'd tow the line because I didn't want to go and work in a factory. But of course I didn't behave. I was suspended several times because I was totally disruptive in class.'

Mary recalls how she tormented her English teacher, Pat Rabbitte, now a Dáil deputy and member of the Democratic Left. 'He was our teacher at the time and I made his life a hell for months. He was doing *Exploring English* [a textbook on the Leaving Cert course] with us and I would have my own ideas and I was constantly contradicting him and asking him awkward questions. I also used to slag him about his name and I'd refer to him as "Bunny". In the end, he left the classroom and told the Reverend Mother he wouldn't go back in till I was removed. So my mother was sent for again.'

During her early teens, Mary admits that she began experimenting with drugs. But the combination of drink and drugs, and the friction at home and in school eventually took its toll on Mary. At fifteen years of age she attempted suicide by taking an overdose of pills and slashing her wrists. She survived and was later treated at the psychiatric hospital in Ballinasloe. 'I spent six weeks in Ballinasloe and it shook me up being in there. I was the only young person in a ward where there were women of sixty or seventy, all kinds of odd-balls. It was a sobering experience. I'll never forget it as long as I live. I never wanted to go back in there again.'

After she was discharged, Mary went back to school. But her behaviour didn't improve. However, she completed the Leaving Certificate examination and ended up with 'a couple of honours'. Two days after completing the exam, Mary ran away from home. She was seventeen.

Her adventure into the world took her initially to Milltown Malbay. 'The Willie Clancy festival was on there at the time and two close friends and myself headed off to it. Then we went on to Lisdoonvarna, Doolin and Lahinch. At that time I knew every traditional song in the book and I used to busk to get money. The other two could do nothing except hold the hat. It was our intention to travel the world, but the other two eventually chickened out and went home after the summer holidays. I made my way up to Limerick where I knew a few people I had met in Galway. They were a particularly arty crowd. At a party there one night I overheard the head of the art department of one of the local colleges complaining how he didn't have live nude models for his students. He had to use statues and photographs. So there and then I said I'd do it. Posing as a nude model became my first job in 1973. The students were embarrassed a lot of the time and I was as well on the first day. But after a while I got used to it. They were very good to me, offering me fags and cups of coffee and putting heaters around me. But it was very boring. I got a one-room flat in Patrick Street and shared a shower and a bathroom with a crowd of Australians who lived in a bigger flat underneath. I had a little garret up at the top of the house. I remember how I painted the floor green and the walls blue. It was paradise. I supplemented my income by working as a part-time waitress in the Galleon Grill. It was my intention to save as much money as possible and to go off around the world.'

Mary eventually moved to London with some friends from Limerick. 'They were going squatting, which was all the rage in England in the seventies. A crowd of us squatted in Ealing. I had various jobs, including one as a street sweeper with the local borough council. I was one of the first women street sweepers to be employed. It was great money and we had a great time. My mother used to send me food parcels because she thought I was starving. And she always sent me a tin of USA biscuits at Christmas.' Mary struck up a relationship in London with a Galway lad and when he returned to Ireland she went with him.

Back in Galway, Mary moved in with her parents. 'That didn't last long. After being used to my freedom I couldn't hack it.' She rented a house with a group of people, including Dutch musician Eric Visser, who was later to produce all her albums. 'He had come to Galway to study O'Carolan. Eric is a classical guitarist. And we all rented a house in Salthill where we passed away the winter.' Her boyfriend, meanwhile, was living at home. In 1975, Mary became pregnant by him and they decided to marry. 'I didn't want to get married but I decided to go ahead with it. Then two days before the wedding I had a miscarriage, so I didn't want to get married at all. But I was convinced it was only my nerves and I should go through with it. The plans were all made. So I did and I became pregnant straight away. Aoife, my first child, was born the following year and the other two children followed quickly after that.' But the relationship didn't work out and the couple split up after six years. Today, she prefers not to go into detail about her relationship with her former spouse. 'These things happen,' she says, shrugging off the question.

Mary recalls working 'at every sort of job when the kids were little'. She was employed by a German knitwear designer in Galway 'for a good many years'. She cleaned windows. She wasn't averse to tackling any form of employment that came her way.

Galway city is a haven for musicians, artists and students. Many of the city's pubs retain an atmosphere that is conducive to 'the craic'. And you'll frequently find a musician in a corner, his or her fingers dancing furiously along the buttons of an accordion, or a frenzied fist pounding a bodhrán, or an arm suspended in mid-air and swiftly gliding over and back across the strings of a fiddle. It was in this environment, performing at seisiúns in the pubs of Galway, that Mary Coughlan's talent began to emerge. People used to tell her she had 'a voice'. She recalls that Dolores Keane was her favourite singer at the time. 'I used to sing all her songs. After her first album came out with

De Danann years and years ago, I started singing the songs that she had covered.'

Eric Visser, her mentor and producer, wrote a tune for Mary's eldest daughter, Aoife, when she was born in 1976. It was a number one hit in the Dutch charts for six weeks and shot Eric and his group Flairck to fame in his homeland. Since then he has been one of the most consistently popular artistes in Holland, with about twenty successful albums to his name. It was Eric who encouraged Mary to develop her talent as a singer and to think in terms of turning professional. It was his influence that drew her more deeply into the genre of jazz. 'I was never into rock 'n' roll or pop music,' Mary says. 'Traditional music was the most accessible thing to me and that's how I started singing. Then I started listening to Billie Holliday, Bessie Smith, Tom Waits and Van the Man [Van Morrison]. And then when Eric wrote songs like "The Beach" and "Lady in Green", which are all on my first album, I demoed them and liked them. I liked the whole feel of that kind of music.'

Mary was twenty-nine years old when she started off her professional career in music, performing with Eric and opening up shows for her established contemporaries, the trilogy of successful Irish female artistes, Mary Black, Maura O'Connell and Dolores Keane. 'Myself and Eric also supported Honor Heffernan and Freddie White, people like that, and that's how I got my name around.' When her debut album, Tired And Emotional, was released in 1985 it made a major impact on the Irish music scene and propelled Mary Coughlan into the public eye. 'The album was Eric's idea. He had written "The Beach" and a few songs like that and he said, "Let's do them. Let's demo them." We didn't have a label or anything, so we just did the album ourselves. Eric paid for it and put it out. Mark Cagney [then a RTE Radio 2 disc jockey and now with the independent radio station, 98FM] was the first person to start playing it on the radio.

'I was totally amazed when Mark Cagney started playing it on the radio,' Mary told Joe Breen of *The Irish Times*. 'My father would ring me up the next day and say, "My God, you were on the radio last night!" I had hoped we would make back the three thousand pounds we had spent on making *Tired And Emotional*, maybe by our friends buying it or whatever. But something occurred to me, I think it was during our second gig in the Harcourt Hotel in Dublin. It was packed to the doors and I was looking down at the audience and saying to myself, "What are they coming here for?" It was a kind of contradiction. I wanted people to come, but I couldn't understand why they had come. The whole thing simply astonished me.' Neither Eric nor Mary had foreseen just how successful the album was to become. It had a phenomenal run of twenty-six weeks in the Irish charts and firmly established Mary Coughlan as a heavyweight artiste. It led to appearances on *The Late Late Show* – a sign that Mary Coughlan had indeed 'arrived'.

Mary then landed a prestigious spot as one of the headline acts at the Cork Jazz Festival. 'That would have been around October/November 1986. I had just put my own band together and that was our first gig together as a group.' Successful tours followed, with the album being critically acclaimed in Britain and Europe. Mary Coughlan was on her way and a whole new life opened up for her and her three young children. By this stage, Mary had long since patched up her differences with her parents and they were now her biggest fans.

The *Irish Times* journalist Joe Breen wrote of how 'Coughlan quickly built up a loyal following for her driving blues and sensitive touch singing, while at the same time her barbed comments on social issues kept her in the headlines. This wild red-haired chanteuse with a penchant for colourful language and strong opinions made excellent copy, so it was no surprise when the British media sought out the stereotype.' She told the *Irish Times*: 'I remember doing an interview, I think it was with the London *Independent,* and the journalist came in looking for this supposedly completely stark raving madwoman with wild red hair. He was in the lobby and I was in the lobby and he didn't recognise me. So, after a while I got fed up waiting for him and I had him paged. And so during the interview he just said, "You know, you're not that bad at all." He probably thought I was going to take a bite out of him because that was what he had been led to believe.'

With Mary's star on the ascent and her career gathering momentum, it seemed inevitable that she would have to establish a base in the capital. So, in 1986 she took the courageous step of uprooting her family from their Galway home, leaving behind her relatives and friends, and moving lock, stock and barrel to Dublin. 'In the beginning, I missed Galway a lot because all my friends were down there,' Mary told *The Sunday World.* 'My children had been going to school there and they had also left behind all their friends. I said to them at the time, "We'll give it two years in Dublin and if we all want to leave, then we will." After a year they didn't want to go back because they found new friends and quickly settled into a new way of life, as children do. They were very young at the time – Aoife was seven, Ollie was five and Eoin was four. We go back to Galway an odd time now to see my parents, or whenever I do a gig down there. That's about it. I went down there every month in the beginning, but now I hardly get the chance at all.'

Following the success of her first album, Mary Coughlan became a household name. Initially, she signed to a small independent record company, Mystery Records, before landing a major contract with East West of the high-powered multinational Warner Music. Her departure from Mystery was a painful experience and gave her her first insight into the murky side of the music industry, the business aspect that can often suffocate an artiste's career. It took two years for the Mystery/East West deal to be sorted out. Two 'lost' years for Mary Coughlan, although she took the opportunity to sample a new experience with a small part in a Neil Jordan film, *High Spirits*. East West released the 1990 album, *Uncertain Pleasures*. Mary's new album featured a star-studded line-up of musicians, including The Communard's Richard Cole, Prefab Sprout drummer Neil Conti and Van Morrison saxophonist Ritchie Buckley. But the album wasn't the sure-fire commercial success that Warner Music had anticipated. 'They spent two hundred thousand pounds doing the album and video and it bombed,' she told *Hot Press*. Then came the 1992 follow-up, *Sentimental Killer*, and suddenly Mary's world fell apart. Her record company weren't impressed and after a six-week run they dropped it. 'They just didn't think that *Sentimental Killer* had any hits on it,' Mary says. She returned triumphant from a fifteen-date tour of Britain to discover that something was amiss on the home front. She told Paul Byrne of *The Irish Press*: '*Sentimental Killer* had been out about six weeks, the reviews had been very good and the tour we'd just done had been great. But when I got back to Dublin it was as if I didn't exist. There was little or no advertising around the town for the album. Not one single poster! When I phoned my record company they told me they didn't believe in postering. Three weeks later there were about ten thousand Christie Hennessy posters all over Dublin – from the same label. They had obviously made up their minds long before they released the album that they really didn't want anything more to do with me.'

Mary and East West went their separate ways and, financially, she was in dire straits. She told Byrne: 'With a major label you're given these big advances every six months. These lovely big cheques just arrive in the post. So last year, when it didn't come, of course it left me in an unreal situation in regard to the house, mortgage, everything. I had already lost one house and I wasn't about to lose this one too.' On that first occasion, Mary had taken out a mortgage on her home in Howth, County Dublin, to finance a tour of Scandinavia. The tour lost eighty thousand pounds and Mary lost the house. Now she was in danger of losing her new home in Bray, County Wicklow, which she had purchased from Neil Jordan. 'I was devastated when the deal fell through,' she told *The Sunday World*. 'I had just bought the house. I was depending on royalty advances which I didn't get. It was very much a slap in the teeth.' The whole sad saga ended up before the courts. 'We went to court and the judge said, "Well, keep paying your money every month." So I've been trying to work to pay that off every month.'

Mary secured a new deal with Demon Records. She set about recording a live album at London's Mean Fiddler rock venue, only to discover that her old record company owned all her songs. 'They would only let me release the album if they got a two and a half per cent over-ride. There was absolutely no way I was going to let them have anything,' she declares. Mary wasn't allowed to re-record or release any part of her back catalogue in any form until her contract expired. She had two years to wait. In the meantime, she came up with a new collection of blues and jazz songs for her latest album, *Love For Sale*. It also includes a song, 'To Love a Man', which she co-wrote with Antoinette Hennessy. 'It was my first time writing,' she told Siobhán Long of *Hot Press*. Does the writing mark a new departure in terms of artistic direction? Is she no longer satisfied with the role of singer? 'We'll wait and see what the reaction is like. Put the toe in,' she laughs.

When Mary's major album deal with East West was suddenly rescinded, she lapsed, not surprisingly, into the depths of depression. To ease the pain and escape the reality of her bleak situation, she turned to the bottle. Alcohol has always been like a time bomb in her life. 'I was very much going through the motions for a long time,' she told *Hot Press*. 'Whenever I got totally broke I'd be thrown into a Midnight at the Olympia gig, which was totally soul-destroying. I still had some pride left in work and going in to play to twelve hundred sloshed people at one o'clock in the morning took every last bit of anything out of me. But I had to do it – I had no house. After living in the lap of luxury in Howth I was now living in the middle of a housing estate in Portmarnock – and pregnant. So, it was basically hell, I'd say, for about two years.' Mary is no longer drinking, she told *Hot Press*. 'I'm off drink now. I can't drink. Well, I know I could drink normally for a few weeks, have a bottle of wine here, a bottle of wine there. A pint here, a pint there. But it's happened to me a few times and it creeps up on you, and you lose your clearheadedness then. I found myself in the situation where I was drinking to anaesthetise myself from pain, which is a natural thing to do, I suppose. I couldn't handle it and I don't think a lot of people realise how dependent on these people [record companies] you get and what I was going through.'

Mary admits that she's still struggling to get her career running at a feasible level. She feels that personnel changes in Demon Records affected the promotion of her last album, *Love For Sale*, which was only released in Ireland and England. 'It's hard to keep going because of the recession and kids aren't buying records. But I'm lucky in that my music is aimed at the over twenty-fives and there's a market there. In Europe, I do really well,' she says. 'I do a lot of business in Germany, Holland, Belgium and Scandinavia. And it's getting bigger all the time. Maybe it has a lot to do with Eric's influence. Irish artistes have a following in those countries, but it's very much an Irish folk thing. I was a bit different. I'm more jazz, which is really what they are into. Eric is very well established in Holland. He has a band over there and they are huge. Anything I do out there is connected to Eric. Any interviews I do out there, he's mentioned in them. He packs a punch.'

There is now stability and harmony in Mary Coughlan's personal life. She has found love and companionship with an Italian-American bio-medical engineer Frank Bonadio, whom she met through a mutual friend one Sunday morning when she went to her local newsagent's to buy the papers. At the time, Frank had never heard of Mary Coughlan. But there was an instant spark between the two and they launched headlong into a trans-Atlantic courtship. Frank was based in Santa Barbara in California but he gave up everything he had there to be with Mary. 'We commuted for a year and then he moved over five years ago. I wasn't prepared to up and move three kids to the States. Frank loves Ireland now. He gets a bit frustrated with the slowness of Telecom Eireann and the monopoly they have and stuff like that, but he's learning to live with it.'

Frank is the father of Mary's youngest child, Clare. And Mary admits that going away on tour and leaving Clare behind is a wrench. 'It's hard because I never left home for more than a night until my next youngest was about six.' Does she feel women have been held back in their careers by the responsibilities of motherhood? 'It depends on the individual. It depends on what you are prepared to sacrifice, either your career or your home life. That's something that men don't have to worry about. The men in this business, or in any business, they leave it up to the women to organise the children. It's a big responsibility trying to get someone to look after your children when you're not around. It's not too bad now because Aoife is nearly eighteen. But it's very hard going away from Clare for three weeks to tour. But I just accept it and she does now. I talk to her every night on the phone. She seems to know. She knows that I come and go now. Frank works, but he's here seven nights a week. It's quite a role reversal. He'd look after her twenty-four hours a day if he had the chance.'

Mary says she would love to be free to marry Frank and finds it frustrating that there is no divorce in this country. 'It doesn't seem like it's going to happen for another few years, but it seems to be going in the right direction. It's been 1987 since the referendum [on whether divorce should be introduced], but I've come to understand a little bit more how the law works. An awful lot of the family law thing will have to change before they ever think about introducing divorce here. Maybe another five years. I'd be hopeful of that. A lot of the people I know go away to Tahiti and places like that to get divorced. But why should you have to incur that expense? I got married here and I would like to be able to get divorced here and marry again if I want to. The lawyers will have a field day when divorce is introduced here. The flood gates will open. I remember the time of the referendum, there were reports of at least seventy-five thousand couples leading separate lives in Ireland and I'd say there are a good many more now. I think the Church has a lot to answer for in the way it handled the whole thing. I think they made a big deal of it down through the years. I think they thought the whole moral fibre of the country was going to fall apart if they introduced contraception and divorce, which is not the case.'

Mary says that she herself is not involved in any organised religion. 'I do believe that there's somebody up there, but I think religion has been divisive down through the centuries. There have been more people killed in God's name. I'm not into organised religion, but I respect people's religion.' Her support for the right of the woman to choose and for the availability of abortion in this country is also well documented. Mary admits that she had an unplanned pregnancy terminated ten years ago. 'I hadn't planned it [the pregnancy] and I didn't feel that I would be able to offer myself completely at that point, and I had three kids. Since then I've had another one. I've been through it and I feel I'm qualified to talk on it. It's a problem that Ireland refuses to face up to. I know what I'm talking about. When I was in the clinic in London, ten of the twelve women were Irish.' A political activist, she supported Mary Robinson in her presidential election campaign. She also campaigned for Minister for the Arts, Culture and the Gaeltacht, Michael D. Higgins, and the Tánaiste, Dick Spring. 'I was disappointed with him [Dick

Spring] initially because I didn't see things changing quickly enough. But maybe they are going about it the right way and maybe change will come and maybe the changes will be more lasting.'

Despite her love/hate relationship with Ireland, Mary Coughlan says she wouldn't live anywhere else. 'I have a great many ardent fans in Ireland,' she recently told *Hot Press*. 'There are also a good many who think I should fuck off and go live elsewhere. But I only answer the questions that I'm asked and I'm a firm believer that people needn't listen to me if they don't want to. They can turn off the radio or not read the paper.' After experiencing the stinging blows that showbusiness can frequently dish out, Mary is reluctant to predict her future on the career front. She says: 'At this stage, I'm really worried about our future because Demon Records haven't taken up the option for another album. My children are incredibly bright at school, fierce honours material altogether. Aoife will probably do a really good Leaving Cert and will want to go to university and so does Ollie. He gets Grade A in everything. And Eoin has gone into all the honours streams in first year in secondary school. So I have all that financial pressure to think about.' However, there are a lot of people supporting her cause. 'Neil Jordan is a great friend and he was pulling out all the stops for me when he was in Los Angeles – giving out my tapes at the Oscars even. So my name is being circulated big-time. We'll just have to wait and see what happens.'

DISCOGRAPHY (albums)

MARY BLACK

TITLE	LABEL/DATE
General Humbert	Dolphin/1975
General Humbert II	Gael Linn/1978
Mary Black	Dara/1983
Song For Ireland - De Danann	Dara/1983
Collected	Dara/1984
Anthem - De Danann	Dara/1985
The Black Family	Dara/1986
Without The Fanfare	Dara/1987
By The Time It Gets Dark	Dara/1989
No Frontiers	Dara/1990
Babes In The Wood	Dara/1991
A Woman's Heart	Dara/1992
The Collection	Dara/1992
The Holy Ground	Dara/1993

FRANCES BLACK

The Black Family	Dara/1986
Time For Touching Home	Dara/1989

After The Ball - Arcady	Dara/1991
A Woman's Heart	Dara/1992
Frances Black & Kieran Goss	CBM/1992

ELEANOR MCEVOY

A Woman's Heart	Dara/1992
Eleanor McEvoy	Geffen Records/1993

DOLORES KEANE

Bonaparte's Retreat - The Chieftains 6	Claddagh/1976
De Danann	Polydor/1977
There Was A Maid	Claddagh/1978
Anthem - De Danann	Dara/1985
Ballroom - De Danann	Warner's/1987
Broken Heart I'll Wander (*Dolores Keane and John Faulkner*)	Mulligan/1979
Farewell To Erin (*Dolores Keane and John Faulkner*)	Mulligan/1980
Sail Og Rua (*Dolores Keane and John Faulkner*)	Gael Linn/1983
The Keane Family (Muintir Catháin)	Gael Linn/1985
The Irish Folk Festival Tour	Mulligan/1980
Folk Friends II	Folk Freak, Germany/ 1981
Dolores Keane	Ringsend Road/1988
Lion In A Cage	Ringsend Road/1989

A Woman's Heart	Dara/1992
Solid Ground	Shanachie/1993
All Heart No Roses (Sean Keane)	Cross Border Media/ 1993

MAURA O'CONNELL

The Star Spangled Molly	Ogham/Shanachie 1981
Maura O'Connell	Ogham/1983
Just In Time	Polydor/Ogham/1986
Western Highway	Polygram/1988
Always	Polygram/1989
A Real Life Story	Warner Bros./1990
Blue Is The Colour Of Hope	Warner Bros./1993

SHARON SHANNON

Sharon Shannon	Solid Records/1991
A Woman's Heart	Dara/1992

MAIRE BRENNAN

Clannad	Philip/1973
Clannad 2	Gael Linn/1975
Dulamán	Gael Linn/1976
Clannad In Concert	Ogham/1978
Crann Ull	Tara/1978
Fuaim	Tara/1981

Magical Ring	RCA/1983
Legend	RCA/1984
Macalla	RCA/1985
Sirius	RCA/1987
The Collection	K-Tel/1987
Past Present	RCA/1989
The Angel & Soldier Boy	RCA/1989
Atlantic Realm	BBC/1989
Anam	RCA/1990
Maire (solo)	RCA/1992
Banba	RCA/1993

MARY COUGHLAN

Tired And Emotional	WEA/1985
Under The Influence	WEA/1987
Uncertain Pleasures	WEA/1990
Sentimental Killer	WEA/1992
Love For Sale	Demon/1993